MACMILLAN READERS

INTERMEDIATE LEVEL

CHARLES DICKENS

David Copperfield

Retold by Elizabeth Walker

MACMILLAN

MACMILLAN READERS

INTERMEDIATE LEVEL

Founding Editor: John Milne

The Macmillan Readers provide a choice of enjoyable reading materials for learners of English. The series is published at six levels – Starter, Beginner, Elementary, Pre-intermediate, Intermediate and Upper.

Level Control

Information, structure and vocabulary are controlled to suit the students' ability at each level.

The number of words at each level:

Starter	about 300 basic words
Beginner	about 600 basic words
Elementary	about 1100 basic words
Pre-intermediate	about 1400 basic words
Intermediate	about 1600 basic words
Upper	about 2200 basic words

Vocabulary

Some difficult words and phrases in this book are important for understanding the story. Some of these words are explained in the story, some are shown in the pictures, and others are marked with a number like this: ...[3]. Words with a number are explained in the Glossary at the end of the book.

Answer Keys

An Answer Key for the *Points for Understanding* section can be found at www.macmillanenglish.com/readers

Contents

A Note About This Story

Charles Dickens wrote his novel, *David Copperfield* (1849–50) in monthly parts. Later, these parts were put together and published as a book. The novel was very successful and Dickens himself said that it was his favourite story.

David Copperfield begins in the 1820s and is told by its hero, David Copperfield himself. David promises to give a true account[1] of his life and the story goes backwards and forwards in time. Many of David's memories are unhappy ones, but he makes himself tell the reader about them. Some of David's experiences are autobiographical – they are based on things that had happened to Dickens himself. Dickens, like David, was sent to work in a factory when he was a small boy.

Some characters in the book are based on real people. For example, Mr Micawber, who is always in debt[2], is a portrait[3] of Charles Dickens' own father.

Novels tell us a great deal about the society in which they are set[4]. This society may be very different from our own. For example, travel was slower in the 1820s, because horses were the only form of transport. People rode horses, or they travelled in vehicles which were pulled by horses. When people wished to travel long distances, they paid to go in a public coach[5]. Rich people had carriages and horses of their own. In country areas, people and their things travelled by carrier's cart[6].

In the 1820s, English society was divided into three parts: upper class, middle class, and lower, or working class. These divisions exist in England today but they are less important now.

All upper and middle class families had servants, who came from the working class. Charles Dickens belonged to the middle class and David Copperfield is a middle class hero. David is successful because he is honest and works hard. He has friends of all classes. The working class Peggottys are David's friends.

They know that he is different from themselves and they accept this. But poor little Emily cannot accept the difference between David and her family. She wants to be a lady, but this is impossible. James Steerforth is the only upper class character in this book. He is rich and clever. But he wastes[7] his own life and ruins[8] other peoples' lives too.

In English society at that time, women were not equal to men. Men believed that women were less intelligent and they could not be as successful. Some women were happy about that because they wanted someone to look after them. Women who did marry were expected to obey their husbands. If they were badly treated[9], no one wanted to help them. People thought that unmarried women were failures.

Children often had difficult and unhappy lives. Thousands of young children did dirty and dangerous jobs. They were often badly treated at home and there were no laws against this. Some children never went to school and few people cared. Many schools were very bad indeed. Children often lived in (or boarded at) schools, because their parents did not want them at home. The masters were often cruel and the teaching in their schools was very bad.

Dickens tried to improve the society in which he lived. He wrote about bad things because he wanted everyone to know the truth. People of all classes read Dickens' stories and enjoyed them. Then they helped Dickens to change society and make their country a better place to live in.

The Places in This Story

1

My Early Days

My name is David Copperfield and I was born in the county[10] of Suffolk, in the east of England. This book is the story of my life. Will I be the hero of my own story? You must read it and decide for yourself.

I never knew my father. He died before I was born. When this story begins, my mother had been a widow[11] for six months. She was living in our big old house in a little village called Blunderstone. One afternoon in March, my mother was sitting by the fire, crying quietly to herself. Her baby would be born soon – a baby that would never know its father. My mother felt lonely and sad.

The room was very quiet. Then, suddenly, there was a tapping sound at the window. My mother, who was easily frighened, looked up quickly.

There was an old lady in the garden. She was looking in at the window, with her face pressed against the glass. My mother stood up and her heart began to beat very fast. She was so frightened, that she almost fainted.

'Who is it? What do you want?' she whispered.

The old lady, who was tall and thin, tapped on the window again. She was wearing spectacles and her bonnet[12] was very old-fashioned. My mother, who had now recogized the old lady, hurried to open the front door.

The old lady spoke first.

'You must be Clara – Mrs David Copperfield,' she said in a sharp voice. 'I am Miss Trotwood – Miss Betsy Trotwood. We haven't met before. But I'm sure you have heard of me. I am your late husband's aunt.'

'Yes, yes, of course,' my mother replied. 'Please come in.'

Miss Betsy Trotwood followed my mother into the sitting-room and sat down by the fire.

'Your husband told you about me, didn't he?' the old lady asked.

My mother nodded. 'Yes, he did,' she said. 'My dear husband – your nephew – often talked about his Aunt Betsy. He spoke of you just before he ... died.'

My poor mother began to cry again.

'Well, here I am,' Miss Betsy said. 'Sit down, child. Let me look at you.'

My mother was very pretty, with a sweet, pale face and long, fair curls.

Aunt Betsy shook her head sadly and gently touched my mother's pretty hair. 'When are you expecting your child[13]?' the old lady asked. 'You are not much more than a baby yourself.'

My mother began to cry more than ever. 'Very soon,' she said. 'I am so frightened. I am afraid that I shall die and my baby too!'

'Nonsense,' Miss Betsy said. 'You won't die and neither will your little girl.'

'The baby may be a boy,' my mother said quietly.

'I don't think so,' Miss Betsy replied. 'I'm sure that the baby will be a girl. Her name will be Betsy Trotwood Copperfield. I will help you look after her, I will teach her to think for herself!'

'Thank you,' my mother whispered. 'I am feeling rather faint,' she went on. 'Do you think ...?'

'Of course, you need a cup of tea. I'll call your servant. What's her name?'

'Peggotty.'

'Peggotty? Who gave her that strange name?' my Aunt Betsy asked.

'It's her family name,' my mother explained. 'Her first name is Clara, like mine. So we ... I ... call her Peggotty.'

My aunt shook her head sadly. Then she got up and opened the door. 'Peggotty!' she called. 'Bring some tea! Mrs Copperfield is not well!'

Peggotty arrived a few minutes later with tea and some lighted candles. Peggotty stared at my aunt and then looked anxiously[14] at my mother.

'Something has upset you, ma'am,' Peggotty said.

'Oh, Peggotty,' my mother replied. 'I feel very ill. I was not expecting Miss Trotwood and she frightened me a little.'

Then my mother gave a cry of pain. 'Oh, Peggotty, help me,' she whispered.

Peggotty ran to my mother and held her hand.

'I think the baby's coming early,' my poor mother went on. 'Oh, Peggotty! The pain! It hurts so much!

'Don't worry, ma'am,' Peggotty said. 'My nephew's in the kitchen. I'll send him for the doctor at once.'

When the doctor arrived, my mother was upstairs in her bedroom with Peggotty. Miss Betsy Trotwood stayed downstairs. She knew nothing about babies.

Soon my mother began to cry out in pain, over and over again. Miss Betsy took off her bonnet and put cotton wool[15] in her ears. Sometimes she sat by the fire. Sometimes she walked up and down the room, holding her bonnet by its strings.

At half past twelve, the doctor came downstairs. He was smiling happily. He bowed[16] to my aunt politely.

'I have good news, ma'am,' he said. 'Mother and baby are both well.'

'What? What did you say?' my aunt shouted, taking the cotton-wool out of her ears.

'It's good news,' the doctor repeated. 'Mrs Copperfield is resting and the baby is healthy. He –'

'*He*? What do you mean?' Miss Betsy cried. 'The baby's a *girl*. She must be. Her name is Betsy Trotwood Copperfield!'

'Ma'am, the baby is a boy,' the doctor said quietly.

My aunt stood up, swung her bonnet by its strings and hit the doctor hard on the head.

'Boys cause nothing but trouble!' she cried. Then she put the bonnet on her own head, walked out of the house and never came back.

My earliest memories are of two women – my dearest mother and dear Clara Peggotty. They both loved me very much. I remember that my young mother had a pale face and soft, pretty hair. Peggotty's eyes and hair were very dark. Her face and arms were hard and red. I think that my mother and I were both a little afraid of Peggotty. But she was a kind woman and we loved her too.

The three of us lived together for seven happy years. During that time, I learnt to read. I read all my dead father's story books again and again. And I was the hero of every story!

I remember the warm summers in our garden. There was an empty dog kennel[17] at one end and sweetly-smelling flowers grew everywhere. In the autumn, my mother and I picked fruit in the garden. In winter, we stayed indoors. I remember my mother dancing by herself in the candle-light. I remember the light shining on her pretty hair.

Then, one day, a tall, black-haired man came to see my mother. He stayed for about half-an-hour. He kissed my mother's hand before he left and put his hand on my head. I did not like that and I moved away from him. Then he looked down at me with his hard, dark eyes and I felt afraid.

As time went on, the black-haired gentleman came nearly every day. His name was Mr Edward Murdstone and he was always very polite. He praised my mother's beauty and made her blush[18]. I hated him for it and I think that Peggotty hated him too.

One evening, when Peggotty and I were alone she spoke to me gently. 'Master Davy[19],' she said. 'Would you like to visit my brother's house in Yarmouth? I'll go with you and we could stay for two weeks.'

'Is your brother a nice man, Peggotty?' I asked.

'Oh, he's *such* a nice man. The nicest I know!' she exclaimed. 'He lives near the sea. You've never seen the sea, Master Davy. There'll be boats and fishermen and my nephew, Ham, lives there too.'

'But what about mama?' I asked. 'She can't live here by herself, can she?'

'Of course not,' Peggotty said quickly. 'Your dear mother will be staying with some neighbours.'

That made me happy and my mother looked happy too.

Peggotty and I were going to travel to Yarmouth in the carrier's cart. As the carrier put our boxes on his cart, my mother stood at the garden gate. She had come to say goodbye to us. I was happy to be leaving, but I suddenly began to cry. Then my mother cried too and I kissed her.

I got into the cart with Peggotty and looked back. Mr Murdstone was standing beside my mother now. She ran after the cart to kiss me one last time. Mr Murdstone frowned[20] but he could not stop her. My dear mother was laughing and crying at the same time.

The carrier's old horse began to pull the cart along the road. I waved[21] goodbye to my mother, as I looked back at my happy home. I did not know then that I would never be happy there again.

2

Friends and Enemies

The carrier's old horse was very slow and our journey to Yarmouth took a long time. Peggotty's nephew, Ham, was waiting for us there. He was a big, tall young man and very strong. He carried me and my box on his shoulders very easily.

We walked through the town and everything there smelt strongly of fish. At last, we came to an open place and Ham stopped.

'There's our house, Master Davy,' he said.

I could see the beach, and beyond it, the sea. But there was no house anywhere. Then I saw an old, black boat that had been pulled up onto dry ground. But this boat had a flat roof and the roof had a metal pipe with smoke coming out of it. There was a door and some little windows in the side of the boat too.

'Is that boat your house?' I asked.

'That's it, Master Davy,' Ham replied, smiling happily.

I was delighted.

Three people were waiting at the door to welcome us. They were Mr Peggotty – our Peggotty's brother – a thin, sad-looking woman, and the prettiest little girl that I had ever seen.

'I'm glad to see you, sir,' Mr Peggotty said to me. 'Come inside.'

The strange little house was very neat and very clean. When we were all inside, there was just room for everyone. Peggotty showed me my own little bedroom. Very soon, we had eaten our supper and were all sitting together round the fire.

By then, I knew everyone's name. The sad-looking woman was Mrs Gummidge, whose husband had been drowned at sea.

'Is that boat your house?'

The pretty girl was little Emily. Ham and little Emily were Mr Peggotty's nephew and niece. Their fathers had both been drowned at sea too.

I began to think that the sea was a cruel and dreadful place. It had killed so many people. Later, when I lay in bed, I listened to the sound of the wind and the waves[22]. I felt afraid.

In the morning, I walked on the beach with little Emily. The pretty little girl was wearing a blue dress. It was the same colour as her eyes.

'I suppose that you love the sea,' I said.

'Love it? No, I'm afraid of it,' little Emily replied. 'The sea is cruel. It kills people. It killed my father.'

'Do you remember him?' I asked quietly and she shook her head. 'My father died before I was born,' I said quickly. 'So you and I are alike.'

Little Emily shook her head again. 'No,' she said. 'We're very different. Your father was a gentleman and your mother's a lady. My father was only a fisherman, and so is my uncle.'

'But Mr Peggotty is a good man,' I said.

'Of course he is!' said little Emily. She laughed. 'If I ever become a lady, I'll buy him a fine blue coat with gold buttons. And a gold watch too.'

'Would you like to be a lady?' I asked.

'More than anything,' she replied. 'Now, watch me!'

As she spoke, the little girl jumped up onto a wooden wall that went out into the sea.

'Be careful!' I cried. 'You'll fall!'

Little Emily laughed again. She ran along the narrow wall to where the sea was coming in on either side.

Little Emily was very happy that day, but her life would be very sad. Of course, we did not know that then.

I watched, as little Emily ran back along the wall. When she jumped down, I kissed her. I was in love!

Two weeks went by very quickly. It was soon time for me to return home with Peggotty. I wanted to see my mother again, but I was sad to leave little Emily. And I was sad to leave Mr Peggotty's strange house and the kind people who lived there.

Peggotty and I travelled in the carrier's cart again. As we got nearer to Blunderstone and my home, I got more and more excited.

'Mama will be very happy to see us!' I cried. 'She'll be at the gate to meet us, won't she, Peggotty?'

Peggotty did not answer. She looked worried and sad, but I did not understand why.

At last, the cart stopped outside our house. I jumped down and opened the garden gate. The door of the house opened, but a new servant stood there, not my mother.

I suddenly felt afraid. I turned towards Peggotty. 'Isn't mama home yet?' I asked.

'Yes, yes, she's home,' Peggotty said quickly. 'Come into the kitchen, Master Davy. I've got something to tell you.'

'Oh, she's not dead, is she, Peggotty?' I cried. 'Please say that mama is not dead!'

'No, your mother's not dead,' Peggotty replied. 'But you … you've got a new father. Come and see him, Master Davy.'

'I don't want to see him!'

'But you want to see your mother, don't you?'

Peggotty opened the door of the sitting-room and pushed me inside. On one side of the fire sat my mother and opposite her was the dark-haired man – Mr Murdstone!

My mother stood up slowly. She looked at Mr Murdstone. Then, smiling, she ran to kiss me.

Mr Murdstone frowned. 'Remember what I told you, Clara,' he said. 'You must not spoil[23] the boy. Be firm[24], my dear, be firm.'

My mother sat down again by the fire. No one told me to sit down. Very soon I left the room.

Everything in the house was different now. Upstairs, I had a new bedroom. It was smaller than my old one and further away from my mother's room. I went downstairs again and walked slowly into the garden. Things had changed there too. There was a big black dog in the kennel and it reminded me of Mr Murdstone. The dog was attached to the kennel by a long metal chain. The dog snarled and barked[25] and its chain rattled.

I went sadly indoors and up to my new bedroom. I lay on the bed and cried until I fell asleep.

Some time later I heard a soft voice say, 'Here he is!'

I opened my eyes and saw my mother and Peggotty.

'Davy, what's the matter?' my mother asked.

'Nothing,' I replied, and turned my head away.

'Davy, Davy my child,' she whispered.

But I would not answer her.

'Look what you've done, Peggotty!' my mother cried. 'You've made my own child hate me because I married again. I needed someone to look after me. I only wanted to be happy!'

'But I want that too, Mrs Copperfield!' Peggotty replied. 'I want us *all* to be happy, you know that.'

At that moment, I felt a heavy hand on my shoulder. I sat up quickly. When I saw Mr Murdstone, I stood up at once.

'Now, Clara, you are not being firm with the boy,' Mr Murdstone said. 'Go downstairs. I want to speak to David alone.'

He kissed my mother and she smiled and left the room. I knew then that she would always obey him.

Mr Murdstone turned to Peggotty and frowned. 'I heard you call my wife by a name that is not hers,' he said. 'She is Mrs *Murdstone* now. Please remember that.'

When Peggotty had gone, Mr Murdstone sat down on a chair and pulled me towards him. His black eyes looked into mine. 'David,' he said, 'if my horse or dog does not obey me, what do I do?

My heart began to beat very fast. 'I don't know,' I replied.

'I beat him,' Mr Murdstone said. 'I beat him hard and I hurt him. Then he obeys me. You understand me, I know. Now wash your face, David, and then come downstairs. My sister, Miss Jane Murdstone, will be here soon. She will want to see you.'

Miss Murdstone arrived later that evening. She was dressed all in black and she had black hair and eyes, like her brother. Her face was hard, like his. She carried a hard metal bag, on a chain. The chain reminded me of the black dog outside in the garden.

'Is this your boy, sister-in-law[26]?' Miss Murdstone asked my mother in a hard voice.

'This is Davy,' my mother replied quietly.

Miss Murdstone looked at me and frowned. 'I don't like boys,' she said.

It was soon clear that Miss Murdstone was not going away. The next day, she asked my mother for the keys to every room and cupboard in the house. She kept the keys in her bag and they rattled there like the black dog's chain.

'I'll be looking after the house now, Clara,' Miss Murdstone said. 'You are too pretty and too impractical[27] to do it.'

'But I looked after the house when –' my mother began.

Miss Murdstone held up her hand to stop her speaking.

'Things are different now,' Miss Murdstone said firmly. 'You are not practical, Clara. I am. My brother and I will look after everything,' she said.

My mother's eyes filled with tears, but she nodded her head. 'Yes, of course, Jane,' she said. 'I am very grateful[28].'

3

I Am Sent Away

My life was now very unhappy. I was never alone with my mother, and Peggotty had to stay in the kitchen. Mr and Miss Murdstone talked about sending me away to school. But meanwhile, I was taught at home.

Before the Murdstones had arrived, my mother had taught me. She was gentle and kind. We read the lesson-books together and my mother explained everything.

I tried hard to learn each lesson. When dear mama asked me to repeat it, I remembered every word.

Now things were very different. Mr Murdstone and his sister were always in the room with us. When I saw their hard faces, I forgot everything that I had learnt so carefully. If my poor mother tried to help me, Mr Murdstone frowned and Miss Murdstone shook her head.

'Oh Davy, Davy,' said my mother sadly.

'Now, Clara,' Mr Murdstone said. 'David has either learnt the lesson or he hasn't.'

'He hasn't,' Miss Murdstone said. 'Give him back the book and *make* him learn it!'

'Yes, do try to learn it, Davy,' my mother said. 'Please don't be stupid.'

Of course, that day I was very stupid and I could not remember anything at all. My mother tried to whisper the right words and the Murdstones saw her. Mr Murdstone stood up at once, took the book and hit me on the head with it. Then Miss Murdstone gave me a long list of figures to add together. I tried to do the sum, but I never got the right answer.

One morning, when I went into the sitting-room with all my

books, my mother was looking very worried. Miss Murdstone's face was hard. Mr Murdstone was holding a thin cane[29]. He moved it about quickly. It made an unpleasant sound which frightened me very much.

'Now, David,' Mr Murdstone said, 'you must be extra careful today.'

He put down the cane and picked up the first book. I tried hard to repeat the words that I had learnt so carefully. But I could not remember any of them. The words *I* said were all wrong. When Mr Murdstone put down the last book and picked up his cane, my mother began to cry.

'Look! You have upset your mother, David,' Mr Murdstone said to me. 'We have tried kindness and now we must try something else. Come with me, boy.'

Mr Murdstone took me, very slowly, upstairs to my room. When we were there, he suddenly twisted[30] my head under his arm.

'Mr Murdstone, sir, please don't beat me!' I cried. 'I can't remember anything when you and Miss Murdstone are in the room, sir! I really can't!'

'You can't? We'll see about that!' he said.

Mr Murdstone hit me once with the cane. It hurt so much that I turned my head and bit his hand.

Then he beat me very hard and I thought that he was going to kill me. He shouted as he beat me. I screamed and cried. I heard my mother and Peggotty crying too.

At last the beating stopped. Mr Murdstone went away, locking my bedroom door behind him.

I lay on my bed in great pain. I felt very wicked – I had bitten my new father! What would happen to me? Would I be sent to prison?

For the next five days, I saw no one but Miss Murdstone. She sometimes gave me some bread and milk. Sometimes, she let me walk by myself in the garden. I wanted to speak to my mother, but she was kept away from me. I was always locked in my room at night. In the middle of the fifth night, I woke up suddenly. Someone was whispering my name. I sat up.

'Is that you, Peggotty?' I whispered back. 'Where are you?'

My name was whispered again. Peggotty was outside the room. She was trying to speak to me through the keyhole. I got out of bed and ran to the door.

'Peggotty, my dear Peggotty!' I cried through the keyhole.

'My own dear Davy, be as quiet as a mouse or the Cat will hear us!' Peggotty said. I knew that she meant Miss Murdstone.

'How is mama?' I asked. 'Is she very angry with me?'

'Not very,' Peggotty replied. 'She's very sorry for you.' Then Peggotty began to cry and, soon, I was crying too.

'What is going to happen to me?' I asked.

'School. Near London,' Peggotty whispered.

'When?'

'In the morning. You'll see your mother before you go. I'll look after her, Davy dear, and I'll write to you.'

'Send my love to my friends in Yarmouth,' I said. 'Tell them that I am sorry.'

'I will, Davy, I will,' Peggotty whispered. 'Go to sleep now, my own dear boy.'

The next morning, at breakfast, I saw only Miss Murdstone and my dear mother. Mama was crying and that made me cry too.

'Why did you hurt someone I love?' she said sadly. 'You have been very bad, but I forgive you, Davy. School will help you. I know that it will. You will be a better boy when you come home in the holidays. Goodbye, my child. God bless you!'

And then the carrier was at the gate. My box was lifted into the cart and I got in too. I was crying now. The carrier's old horse began to move forward and I was carried slowly away from my home.

About half a mile down the road, Peggotty was waiting for

us. She climbed onto the cart with several bags of little cakes. She put the bags on the seat beside me and gave me a little purse too. Then she kissed me, got down from the cart, and went back up the road.

I looked inside the purse. There was some money from Peggotty and some more from my mother. My mother had also written a note. It said: *For Davy, with my love.*

I began to cry again and soon my handkerchief[31] was very wet. Then I thought about the heroes of my favourite stories. I remembered that they never cried. So I tried very hard to stop crying.

I offered Mr Barkis – that was the carrier's name – a cake and ate one myself.

'Did *she* make them?' Mr Barkis asked.

'Do you mean Peggotty?'

'Yes. Her.'

'Oh, yes,' I said. 'She makes our cakes and does all the other cooking. She's a very good cook.'

'She's not married?'

'No, Mr Barkis.'

'Someone *wants* to marry her, perhaps?' the carrier asked.

'I don't think so, Mr Barkis,' I replied.

'Then I want you to tell her that *Barkis* is willing.'

'Can't you tell her yourself, Mr Barkis?' I asked.

'You write to her,' he said. 'Just say – "Barkis is willing[32]." '

After that, I fell asleep. Mr Barkis and his horse were taking me as far as Yarmouth. There, I must wait in the inn[33], for the coach to London.

Next morning, I wrote a letter to Peggotty.

Dear Peggotty,
I have come here safe. I send my love to Mama. I must tell you - Barkis is willing.
Love, Davy.

I did not understand the carrier's message but I hoped that Peggotty would.

The coach for London left Yarmouth at three o'clock in the afternoon. It was summer and the evening was very pleasant. As we drove through the villages, I saw little boys playing together. I thought about their fathers and mothers. Were the boys happy? I hoped so. Sometimes I thought about my new school and then I felt afraid.

The coach went on all through the night. I tried to sleep but I was too cold and uncomfortable. As the sun came up, I could see London. I looked at the great city coming nearer and nearer. What was going to happen to me there? My heart began to beat faster.

4

School

The name of my school was Salem House. When I arrived, the boys and the masters were still away on holiday. There was only one young master there to look after me. Mr Murdstone had sent me to the school early. He was punishing me because I had bitten him.

I walked sadly around the empty classroom and looked at the rows of desks. One morning, I saw a large piece of card on one of the desks. It had some writing on it. It said: TAKE CARE. HE BITES.

'Excuse me, sir,' I said to the master. 'Where is the dog?'

'There is no dog, Copperfield,' the master said. 'That card is for you. I have been told to fix it on your back. You must wear it all the time.'

After a month, the headmaster returned to the school. His name was Mr Creakle and he called me to his room.

Mr Creakle was a red-faced man, with small eyes and a large chin. I soon found out that he never spoke in a loud voice, but always whispered. He stared hard at me and smiled.

'I know your stepfather[34] – Mr Murdstone,' the headmaster whispered. 'He knows me and I know him. You don't know me yet, boy, do you?'

'No, sir.'

Mr Creakle laughed. Then he leaned forward and held me by my ear. 'But soon, you *will* know me,' he said. 'And you'll soon know this too!' As he spoke, he picked up a cane and shook it in front of my face. 'You may go now,' he whispered.

'Please, sir,' I said. 'I am very sorry that I bit your friend, Mr Murdstone. He has already punished me, sir. Please let me take off this card before the boys see it.'

Mr Creakle said nothing. He jumped from his chair and waved his cane at me. I ran from the room, shaking with fear.

Very soon, all the masters and the boys returned to the school. The first boy who spoke to me saw the card on my back. He laughed, but not in an unkind way. He told me that his name was Thomas Traddles.

Some of the other boys laughed when they saw my card, but Traddles stopped them. As time went by, I almost forgot about the card and the boys did too.

The last boy to return to Salem House was tall and very handsome. His name was James Steerforth and he was several years older than me. Everyone said that Steerforth was the cleverest boy in the school. He was very kind to me and he let me sit beside him in the classroom.

'What money have you got, young Copperfield?' he asked, smiling at me.

'But soon, you will know me,' he said.
'And you'll soon know this too!'

I told him that I had seven shillings[35].

'Perhaps I should look after your money for you,' Steerforth said. 'I expect that you'd like to buy some cakes. And something to drink.'

'Well, yes,' I said slowly.

'And fruit and biscuits too,' Steerforth added. 'I'll buy everything for you, don't worry. I'll get as much as I can for your seven shillings, Copperfield. The other boys will be pleased. We can eat the food tonight when the masters have all gone to bed!'

Later that night, Steerforth gave out the food and drink. All the boys enjoyed it very much.

'Good night, young Copperfield,' Steerforth said, as I was falling asleep. 'Don't worry about anything. I'll look after you.'

'Thank you, Steerforth,' I said.

I woke up later and saw Steerforth's handsome face in the moonlight. He was sleeping with his head on one arm and his face was very calm.

I soon found out that Steerforth did what he liked at Salem House. He was never caned. But that gave Mr Creakle more time to cane us and he enjoyed it very much. Poor Traddles was caned every day, but he was always cheerful. I was caned too, but not as much as Traddles.

Salem House was not a good school. There was more caning than teaching there, but somehow, I learnt a little.

One hot afternoon, a servant came into the classroom.

'Visitors for Copperfield,' he said.

I was very surprised. Mr Peggotty and Ham had come to visit me. I was very happy to meet my friends again.

'You've grown tall, Master Davy!' Mr Peggotty cried.

'How are mama and Peggotty?' I asked. 'And what about Mrs Gummidge and little Emily. Are they well too?'

'They're all well, Master Davy,' Mr Peggotty said, smiling. 'Little Emily's nearly a woman now.'

'She's grown so pretty and so clever,' Ham said happily.

Just at that moment, Steerforth walked by and I stopped him.

'These two fishermen are my good friends,' I said. 'They live in a boat, Steerforth.'

'In a boat?' said Steerforth, laughing. 'That sounds the right kind of house for a fisherman! I should like to see it some time, Copperfield.'

'You'd be welcome any time, sir,' Mr Peggotty said. 'Master Davy must bring you with him, when he comes to Yarmouth again.'

'Steerforth has been a good friend to me,' I said. 'Please tell them so at home.'

'I'll ask little Emily to write to my sister,' Mr Peggotty replied.

The rest of the term passed slowly, but at last the holidays came. Soon I was in the Yarmouth coach and on my way home. Mr Barkis and his cart were waiting for me at the inn in Yarmouth the next morning.

'I gave your message to Peggotty, Mr Barkis,' I said. 'Did she give you an answer?'

Mr Barkis shook his head. 'No answer,' he replied. 'I expected an answer.'

When we arrived at the old house in Blunderstone, I expected to see Mr and Miss Murdstone, but they were not there. I went into the house very quietly. I could hear my mother singing, as she had once sung to me. I opened the door to the sitting-room and went inside.

My mother was holding a little baby in her arms. She looked up when she saw me, and smiled. 'My dearest Davy,' she said. 'Come and meet your little brother.'

Then Peggotty came running in and we all laughed and cried together.

The Murdstones were out for the day, so Peggotty had dinner with us. While we were eating, I remembered Mr Barkis.

'Why didn't you give Mr Barkis an answer, Peggotty?' I asked her.

Peggotty blushed and began to laugh and shake her head.

'What's the matter?' my mother asked, laughing too.

'The silly man wants to marry me!' Peggotty replied.

'Oh, please don't leave me!' my mother cried. 'Whatever will I do without you?'

'You dear, silly thing!' Peggotty replied. 'Of course, I won't leave you.'

Then we all laughed again and were very happy. The Murdstones did not return until nearly ten o'clock and I went to bed soon afterwards.

At breakfast, Miss Murdstone stared at me. 'How long are the holidays?' she asked coldly.

'A month, ma'am,' I replied.

'Only a month? That's good,' Miss Murdstone said.

I was never able to see my mother alone and Mr Murdstone never let me sit in the kitchen with Peggotty. So I went for long walks by myself, or I sat in my own room, reading. Then the Murdstones were angry with me and said that I was ungrateful. That made my poor mother cry. But Mr and Miss Murdstone would always make her agree with them.

'Yes, my dear Edward. You must be right,' she always said. Or she answered, 'I'm sure that you know best, Jane.'

So when the holidays ended, I was not sorry to return to Salem House. Mr Creakle would be there with his cane, but I was looking forward to seeing Steerforth again.

On the day I was leaving, Mr Barkis and his cart came to

the garden gate. Now I was sad to be leaving my mother and we both cried.

I sat in the cart and my mother called my name, very softly. She was standing sadly at the garden gate, holding up my baby brother for me to see.

That is how I have always remembered my mother in my dreams. I did not know then that I had lost her.

5

I Begin Work

I can remember very little about the next two months, except that life went on as before. I was used to Salem House now and I expected to stay at the school for many more months.

In March, it was my birthday. It was a cloudy day and very cold. A servant came into the room.

'David Copperfield,' he said. 'Come with me, please!'

I was expecting a box of food from Peggotty, so I got up quickly. I went to the room where Mr Creakle and his wife were eating breakfast. Mrs Creakle had a letter in her hand.

'I have something to tell you, David Copperfield,' she said slowly. 'It is about your mama. She's very ill.'

I looked at Mrs Creakle's sad face and began to shake with fear. I knew what she was going to say and I began to cry.

'I'm afraid that your mama is dead,' she said.

Then I cried and cried. Mrs Creakle was very kind to me and I stayed in her room all day. Later, she told me that my baby brother was very ill too. That made me cry even more.

I went home for my mother's funeral[36]. I did not understand then that I would never go back to Salem House. At Yarmouth,

Mr Barkis was waiting for me as usual. And later, at our garden gate, I saw my dear Peggotty. She held me in her arms and kissed me. She told me that my little brother had died too. He was going to be buried with my mother. The Murdstones were in the house but they did not speak to me.

A few days later, my mother and brother were buried in the same grave. Peggotty and I stood by the grave together. Peggotty cried and I held her hand very tightly. Then I cried too.

After the funeral, Miss Murdstone told Peggotty that she must leave in a month's time. But Miss Murdstone said nothing about me. Mr Murdstone did not speak to me at all. They both left me alone. Neither of them wanted me in the house. But they made sure that I did not see Peggotty.

Good, dear Peggotty soon decided that if Barkis was willing, then she was too. They were married in Yarmouth. I was allowed to go to the wedding. Afterwards, Mr and Mrs Barkis, Mr Peggotty, Ham, Mrs Gummidge, little Emily and I had a meal together. Emily had grown more beautiful than ever. I wished that *we* could be married too.

I returned to the house in Blunderstone and I stayed there with the Murdstones for several months. Peggotty was not allowed to visit me. And the Murdstones would not let me visit Peggotty.

Then, one morning, after breakfast, Mr Murdstone spoke to me. 'I have something to tell you, David,' he said. He stared at me, with his hard, black eyes. Then he spoke again.

'I am not a rich man, David,' he said. 'Education costs a lot of money and I can't afford to spend any more on you. The world is a hard place and it's time that you found that out. You can't go on living here, doing nothing. I've decided that you must start work. You must learn to look after yourself.'

I did not reply. What could I say?

'I have a business partner – Mr Grinby,' Mr Murdstone

went on. 'We own a warehouse[37] in London. We have several boys working there and you are going to join them. You will earn enough for food and drink, with a little money left over. I shall pay for a room and you will live there. Your home will be in London now.'

I was, at that time, just ten years old.

The London warehouse of Murdstone and Grinby was a terrible place. It was at the end of a narrow street that went down to the River Thames. The building was old, damp and dirty and it was full of rats. There were three other boys working there and one of them showed me what to do.

The business sold bottles of wine to ships. When the empty bottles arrived at the warehouse, we had to wash them. When the bottles had been filled with wine again, we put labels on them. Then we carefully put the bottles into wooden boxes. It was hard, boring work and I often thought of Salem House. As I washed the bottles, tears ran down my face and fell into the cold water.

At half past twelve, we stopped for dinner. A fat, middle-aged man, whose head was as bald as an egg, came into the warehouse. He waved his walking stick in the air and walked towards me.

'I believe that you are Master Copperfield, sir,' he said, looking at me through his eye-glass. 'My name is Wilkins Micawber. I hope you are well.'

'Yes, sir, thank you,' I replied. 'I hope you are too.'

Mr Micawber bowed. 'I have had a letter from Mr Murdstone,' he said. 'I work for him sometimes. He suggested that I should take a young gentleman into my humble[38] home. The young gentleman will live with Mrs Micawber, my family and myself. Yes, *you*, Master Copperfield, are to live with us!'

I thanked Mr Micawber, who promised to return for me at eight o'clock that night.

Later, we walked together along the crowded London streets. Mr Micawber talked all the time. He used very long words and sometimes, I found it difficult to understand him. But he was a kind man and he and his wife, Mrs Micawber, soon became my friends.

Mrs Micawber was a pale, thin woman with four children. She was always worrying about her husband and his money problems. Although I was very young, she told me everything.

At the end of every conversation, she said the same words. 'But I shall never leave Mr Micawber!' She made me feel very sorry for her.

Mr Micawber had many great ideas for making money. He was, in his own words, 'always waiting for something to turn up[39]'. But it never did. Mr Micawber never had enough money and he was always in debt.

My own unhappy life went on, day after day. I spent most of my money on food, but I was always hungry. Every morning, I walked to the warehouse. Every evening, I walked sadly back to my room. Every day was the same.

Then, one evening, I returned to the Micawbers' house and found it nearly empty. Mr Micawber had sold most of the furniture, to pay his debts.

Mr Micawber hoped to find a job in Plymouth. The Micawber family was leaving London in a week's time. It was then that a new idea came into my head. I had been thinking about my father's aunt, Miss Betsy Trotwood, for some time. My mother had told me the story of Miss Betsy's visit many times. And my mother had told me how gently the old lady had touched her hair. I did not know where Miss Betsy lived, but I decided that I must find her.

I wrote a letter to Peggotty, asking her to lend me a little money. I also asked her where Miss Betsy lived. But I did not tell Peggotty my plan.

Dear Peggotty sent me the money at once. She told me that

Miss Betsy lived near Dover, a little town by the sea. When the Micawbers left London, I set off alone – along the Dover Road.

6

I Begin a New Life

The journey to Dover was long and hard. Sometime before I left the crowded London streets, most of my money was stolen. I had soon spent my last few pennies. On the second day, I had to sell my jacket to buy food. On the sixth day of my journey, I reached Dover. I was tired and dirty and there were holes in my shoes. I looked like a beggar[40]. Would my aunt believe my story? I did not know, but I knew that I had to find her.

I was on the top of a high, white cliff. I could see the beach and the sea far below. There were some houses on the cliff and a little shop. I went inside.

'Please, ma'am,' I asked the shopkeeper, 'I am looking for Miss Betsy Trotwood. Does she live near here?'

A young woman who was in the shop turned and looked at me. 'Why do you want to see Miss Trotwood?' she asked.

'I want to speak to her, please,' I whispered.

'You want to beg from her, I expect,' the young woman said. 'I'm Miss Trotwood's servant. Follow me, if you want to see her.'

I followed the servant very slowly, as I was very tired. We were soon walking on soft grass. Then I saw a pretty little house, with a garden in front of it. The young woman went through the garden gate and shut it behind her.

'This is Miss Trotwood's house,' she said. Then she went into the house and shut the door.

I stood on the grass outside the garden. I was dirty and tired and I did not know what to do next. Suddenly, the door opened and a tall old lady walked out.

'Go away!' she said. 'We don't want boys here!'

She turned away and began to cut some flowers. I opened the gate very quietly and walked towards her.

'Please, ma'am,' I said. 'Please, *aunt* ...'

Miss Betsy Trotwood turned and stared at me. '*What* did you say?' she cried.

I began speaking very quickly. And as I went on speaking, I began to cry.

'Please, ma'am, I am your nephew, David Copperfield,' I said. 'I have been very, very unhappy since my mother died. I was badly treated and made to work. I ran away, but I lost my money. I have not slept in a bed for five nights.'

'God bless me!' my aunt said and sat down on the garden path. But she soon stood up, took me into the house, and sat me down on a chair.

'Janet!' she called and her servant came into the room. The young woman was very surprised to see me there.

'This boy is my late[41] nephew's son – young David Copperfield,' my aunt said. 'What shall I do with him?'

'Wash him!' Janet replied.

'You are right,' Aunt Betsy said.

Shortly afterwards, I was clean again and wrapped in a warm shawl[42]. I now began to look round the room and at my aunt herself.

My aunt, Miss Betsy Trotwood, was a thin, straight-backed woman who wore spectacles over her sharp eyes. She did not smile very much, but her face was kind. She was neatly dressed in a plain, light-coloured dress.

The room was neat too and everything was very clean. The

window was open and fresh air came into the room. The air smelt of flowers and I could smell the sea too. I was feeling very sleepy now. Someone put me on a couch[43] very gently and covered me with the shawl. As I closed my eyes, I heard my aunt's voice.

'Poor boy, poor little boy,' she said.

Warm and happy, I was soon asleep.

I can remember waking up and having a good meal, which made me sleepy again. Then I was carried up to a neat, clean bedroom with a soft bed. I thought of my dear mother before I fell asleep. And I thanked God that I had found my aunt.

In the morning, I told Aunt Betsy the story of my short life. My aunt shook her head sadly several times. But she said nothing until I had finished.

'I shall have to write to your stepfather, Mr Murdstone,' she said. 'I shall have to tell him that you are here.'

'Oh, please, aunt, don't send me back to him!' I cried. 'He does not want me!'

'We shall soon find out if that is true,' my aunt replied.

After a few days, a letter arrived from Mr Murdstone. It said that he and his sister would visit Miss Trotwood the next day.

By this time, I had found out that my Aunt Betsy Trotwood had some unusual ideas. She hated boys – except for me – and she hated donkeys. 'They are all noisy and dirty,' she said.

People often hired donkeys to ride up to the top of the cliff. And the donkeys were led by boys.

Whenever my aunt saw donkeys on the grass outside her garden, she called her servant. 'Janet! Donkeys!' she cried. Then they would both run onto the grass and make the donkeys go away. I found it very exciting.

On the day of the Murdstones' visit, I sat near the window with my aunt. We could see the pretty garden and the grass beyond it. It was a beautiful day.

The Murdstones did not arrive until late in the afternoon. I saw Miss Murdstone first. And yes, she *was* riding a donkey.

I looked at my aunt quickly. What would she do now?

Miss Murdstone rode slowly across the grass in front of Aunt Betsy's garden. A boy was leading the donkey.

Aunt Betsy stood up.

'Janet!' she called to her servant. 'Donkeys!'

At the same moment, my aunt saw Mr Murdstone, walking slowly towards her.

'Get that animal off the grass, sir!' my aunt cried, as she ran into the garden. 'Get off the grass – both of you! Janet, help me send these people away!'

'That is Mr Murdstone and his sister!' I whispered.

'I don't care who they are,' my aunt replied. 'People don't ride donkeys here and that boy knows it!'

Miss Murdstone got down from the donkey and the boy led the animal away. My aunt walked back into the house and the Murdstones followed her.

'You'd better sit down,' Aunt Betsy said to them.

I was very frightened of Mr Murdstone, who frowned at me as usual.

'Shall I go to my room, aunt?' I asked.

'No, sit here by me,' Aunt Betsy said. 'You are quite safe.'

She turned to Mr Murdstone. 'Now, sir, you wanted to see me,' my aunt said. 'What have you got to say? I am ready to listen.'

'David Copperfield is a bad boy, ma'am,' Mr Murdstone began.

Miss Murdstone nodded her head.

'The boy made trouble between my dear late wife and myself,' Mr Murdstone went on. 'She spoilt him.'

'His mother was not much more than a baby herself,' my aunt said quietly.

'I sent David to school, but he did not change,' Mr

'Get that animal off the grass, sir!'

Murdstone said. 'So I found him work in my own warehouse. Now he has run away!'

'He's bad and ungrateful too,' Miss Murdstone said.

'Did his mother agree with you about her son?' my aunt asked.

'My wife trusted me,' Mr Murdstone replied. 'She agreed with *everything* I said.'

My aunt laughed. 'Your late wife knew nothing about the world,' she said. 'She was only a child when she married you. You frightened her. You made her obey you. Why are you here now?'

Mr Murdstone stood up and frowned. 'I am willing to take the boy back,' he said. 'I shall teach him to obey me. Or do you want to keep the boy, Miss Trotwood? Make up your mind. I shall never come here again.'

My aunt looked at me. 'Do you want to go with them, David?' she asked.

'No, aunt, no!' I cried. 'They were unkind to my mother and they were unkind to me too. Please let me stay here with you!'

My aunt stood up. 'I'll keep the boy,' she said. 'I would not give you my cat to look after, Mr Murdstone. You ruined your poor wife's life. You would like to ruin her son's life too, but I shall not give you the chance. Go now, sir, and you too ma'am,' she said, turning to Miss Murdstone. 'And if you ever ride a donkey on my grass again, ma'am, I'll knock your bonnet off and jump on it!'

Miss Murdstone was too shocked to reply. My aunt watched the Murdstones leave and then turned to me.

'So, your new life begins, David,' Aunt Betsy said. 'I shall call you David Trotwood Copperfield. You have a new life and a new name. And tomorrow, I shall buy you new clothes!'

7

I Begin to Do Very Well

'David, we must think about your education,' my aunt said, a day or two later. 'There are good schools in Canterbury. Would you like to go to school?'

'Oh, yes, aunt. I would like that very much.'

'Then I'll take you to Canterbury tomorrow,' she said. 'It isn't far away.'

My aunt hired[44] a horse and a little carriage. We drove to Canterbury the next day.

'Are you happy now?' she asked me, as we drove along.

'Very happy, aunt,' I said.

It was busy in Canterbury and the streets were crowded with carts and people. We stopped outside a very old house with long narrow windows.

'Is this the school, aunt?' I asked.

'No, this is Mr Wickfield's office and his house too. Mr Wickfield is my lawyer. I want his advice. We'll stop here first.'

I saw a young man's face looking at us through one of the windows. The face, which was very long and thin, disappeared. A few moments later, the door opened and the young man, who had very short, red hair, let us in. He was dressed in black and he moved his long, thin body in a strange way.

'Is Mr Wickfield here, Uriah Heep?' my aunt asked the young man.

'Yes. Mr Wickfield is in his office,' Uriah Heep said. 'Please come in.'

Mr Wickfield had white hair and a rather red, but handsome face. He was smartly dressed and he looked honest and kind. He bowed and smiled when he saw my aunt.

'How can I help you, Miss Trotwood?' he asked her politely.

'This boy is my late nephew's son. His name is David Trotwood Copperfield,' Miss Trotwood replied. 'I need to find a school for him. He would have to live in Canterbury, of course.'

'Dr Strong's school is the best in the city,' Mr Wickfield replied. 'I'll take you there and you can look at it.'

Mr Wickfield smiled at me. 'This young man can wait here in my office,' he said.

Uriah Heep, who was Mr Wickfield's clerk[45], was working in a smaller office. Every time I looked up, he was staring at me with his little red-brown eyes. I walked round the room but the clerk was always watching me. He made me feel very afraid.

After some time, Mr Wickfield returned with my aunt. She had been very pleased with the school.

But she had not found a place for me to stay.

'I think that I can help you with that,' Mr Wickfield said. 'Your nephew can stay here.'

'But —' my aunt began.

Mr Wickfield held up his hand. 'I know what you are going to say,' he said, smiling. 'You can pay me a little money for your nephew's room and his food.'

'Of course,' Aunt Betsy said. 'Thank you. I'm sure that David will be happy here.'

'Then come and meet my little housekeeper[46],' Mr Wickfield replied.

He took us upstairs, into a pretty sitting-room. The room was full of books and flowers. There was a piano in one corner and a young girl was playing it. She stood up, ran towards Mr Wickfield, and kissed him.

'This is my little housekeeper, my daughter Agnes,' Mr Wickfield said.

Agnes smiled. Her happy face, as always, was quiet and calm.

Agnes showed me my room and my aunt and I were delighted with it. As I was starting school the next day, my aunt left me at the Wickfields' house.

'I'll send your things here tomorrow,' Aunt Betsy said. 'Work hard, David.'

'Yes, aunt,' I replied.

I had dinner with Mr Wickfield and his daughter that night, and every night. I could see that Mr Wickfield loved Agnes very much. He smiled whenever he looked at her calm, sweet face. I also saw that he drank too much wine and that sometimes the wine made him sad and forgetful.

One evening, I saw a light shining in Uriah Heep's office. I decided to talk to him.

'You are working late, Uriah,' I said.

He smiled strangely before he replied. 'I am learning about the law, Master Copperfield,' he said.

'I see,' I said. 'You want to be a lawyer.'

'You are right, Master Copperfield,' Uriah replied. 'Of course, I am only a humble clerk *now*. But Mr Wickfield will help me, I'm sure.'

'Then one day, perhaps, he'll make you his partner,' I said,

'Oh, no, Master Copperfield. I am much too humble for that,' Uriah said. But at that moment he did not look humble at all. 'Humble' was Uriah's favourite word and he always used it about himself. And when he used the word, he twisted his thin body, like a snake.

'I suppose that you will be staying here, Master Copperfield,' Uriah went on. 'Miss Agnes will look after you and you will be very happy, I'm sure. She's a sweet young lady, isn't she?' He smiled again and he twisted his body. I was glad when he went home.

My new school was very different from Salem House. Doctor Strong – the headmaster – was a kind and gentle man. With his help, I did very well.

I wrote to Peggotty and returned the money that she had lent me. She sent me many letters, giving me all the news about her family in Yarmouth. She also told me that the Murdstones had gone away from Blunderstone and that our old house was empty.

Sometimes my aunt came to Canterbury to see me. She was pleased that I was happy and working hard at school.

Uriah Heep was always very polite to me, but I did not know if I liked him or not. One day, he invited me to his home. He wanted me to meet his mother. Mrs Heep looked exactly like her son – she was thin, red-haired and very humble. As I drank some tea with them, they asked me questions about Mr Wickfield and his business. Their questions were very clever and I told them far too much. Then Uriah began to talk about Agnes.

I began to feel very uncomfortable. Finally I stood up and told them that I had to leave.

As I was going out of the door, I saw a fat, bald man walking down the street. It was my old friend, Mr Micawber!

'Copperfield! Is that you?' Mr Micawber cried, waving his walking stick at me.

We shook hands and Uriah watched us with his little red-brown eyes.

'Any friend of Master Copperfield's is a friend of mine,' the clerk said. 'Please walk into my humble home, sir. Please come and meet my mother.'

I did not want Uriah to talk to Mr Micawber. Uriah would ask him too many questions about me. He would find out about my time in Mr Murdstone's warehouse.

I smiled at Mr Micawber. 'Shall we go and see Mrs Micawber, sir?' I asked.

'Mrs Micawber will be delighted to see you,' Mr Micawber replied. 'Follow me. Our new home is not far away.'

Mrs Micawber *was* very happy to see me. I soon found out that nothing had 'turned up' for Mr Micawber in Plymouth. He was now hoping to find work in Canterbury. Mrs Micawber told me once more that she would never leave Mr Micawber. Then she invited me to dinner in a few days' time.

When we met again, Mr Micawber looked very happy. He had several new ideas for making money. He told me that he had visited Uriah and his mother. That worried me, but I said nothing.

Then, only two days later, I received a long letter from Mr Micawber. He owed money and he had no way of paying the debt. The Micawbers had to leave Canterbury at once, before Mr Micawber's creditors found him. The letter was signed: *That unhappy beggar, Wilkins Micawber.*

I went to the Micawbers' house to say goodbye to them. But I was too late. As the London coach drove by, I saw that it was carrying Mr Micawber and his family back to the great city again. They were all smiling happily and did not see me. Perhaps 'something had turned up', at last.

The days passed pleasantly at Dr Strong's school. Months went by and then years. I did well and, at the age of seventeen, I became head boy[47]. Then, suddenly, I was grown up. My school days were over and I had to think about a career[48].

8

I Meet Old Friends

I was not sure what I wanted to do. What was my career to be? My aunt and I talked about it many times.

'I have an idea, David,' my aunt said, one evening. 'Why don't you take a holiday before you decide? You could visit your friends in Yarmouth. Take the London coach from Canterbury and stay in London for a day or two.'

I liked this idea. Aunt Betsy and I agreed that I should take three or four weeks holiday. I left Dover with some money from my aunt, and a box full of new clothes.

Before I left Canterbury, I went to say goodbye to the Wickfields. I spoke to Agnes first.

'I shall miss you, my dear sister,' I said. 'I always think of you as a sister, Agnes. You have been so good and so helpful to me. If ever I am in trouble, or fall in love, I shall come to you. I'll ask you for advice. I hope that you will ask me for advice too.

'In fact, I'm surprised that you are not in love by this time,' I went on. 'Or perhaps someone loves *you*, Agnes dear.'

Agnes blushed and shook her head. Then she spoke quietly. 'I am very worried about papa,' she said. 'Have you seen any change in him lately?'

'Yes. I'm afraid I have,' I said. 'Your father is drinking more wine than he did before. Sometimes his hands shake and sometimes he cannot speak clearly.'

'And those are times when Uriah asks him about business,' Agnes said sadly. 'Papa tells Uriah too much. Then my father is sorry and he drinks even more.'

At that moment, Mr Wickfield came slowly into the room and I said goodbye to him.

Last of all, I said goodbye to Uriah Heep. He was pleased to see me go, I was sure.

Soon I was on the coach and travelling fast along the London road. I was well-educated, well-dressed and I had plenty of money. I thought of the past. I remembered walking along that same road, years before. How my life had changed!

The coach drove past Salem House School and I remembered Mr Creakle and his cane. And I thought about Thomas Traddles and James Steerforth. Where were they now?

At last, the coach arrived in London. I went to an inn and was shown to my room. It was a very small room but I felt very excited to be there. I was a young man, by myself in the great city.

The next two days passed very pleasantly. I went to the theatre. I dined in good restaurants. I walked along the crowded streets of London and I felt very happy.

When I returned to the inn on the second evening, I heard a voice that I knew. A handsome, well-dressed young man was talking to a servant.

'Steerforth!' I cried. 'I am so glad to see you here!'

The young man turned, looked at me for a moment, and then smiled. 'It's young Copperfield!' he said. 'What are you doing here?'

'I am on my way to Yarmouth,' I replied. 'What about *you*?'

'I am studying at Oxford now,' Steerforth replied. 'But the university is a dull place. I often come to London.'

'Why don't you come to Yarmouth with me?' I asked. 'You met Mr Peggotty, the fisherman, when he came to Salem House. And I have told you about his sister, Peggotty, who used to look after me.'

'Yes, I remember her strange name,' Steerforth said, smiling.

'When are you going to Yarmouth?' Steerforth went on.

'Tomorrow.'

'Then we'll go together,' said Steerforth happily.

When I was at school, James Steerforth was my hero. He was very kind to me and I was grateful. Now that I had seen him again, my feelings had not changed. James Steerforth was handsome and clever. He was polite to everyone and I was proud that he was my friend.

Our coach journey to Yarmouth passed very pleasantly. I left Steerforth at the inn and went alone to see Peggotty – or Mrs Barkis as her name was now. At first, she did not recognize me and then she held out her arms.

'Davy! My darling boy!' she cried, and we both began to cry.

Mr Barkis was not well, but he was glad to see me too. I told Peggotty that my school friend, Steerforth, was with me. He came to the house later and we all had dinner together. Steerforth told us stories and made us laugh. We all enjoyed ourselves very much.

Later that evening, I took Steerforth with me to Mr Peggotty's house. As we walked together through the darkness, the wind was blowing strongly.

'It's a wild kind of place, isn't it?' I said.

'It is,' Steerforth replied. 'And the sea sounds like a hungry animal. I can see a light over there. Is that the boat where the fisherman's family lives?'

'Yes, that's it,' I said. 'Let's go quietly. I want to surprise them!'

As I opened the door, everyone in the room turned towards us. There was a moment of silence, and then everyone began talking at once.

'Master Davy! It's Master Davy!' Ham cried.

'Master Davy and his friend too!' Mr Peggotty said, as he came forward to welcome us. 'I remember visiting you at school. You have grown into a fine young gentleman.'

Little Emily did not speak, but she smiled at me. When she saw Steerforth looking at her, she blushed and turned away.

'This is a great night for us all,' Mr Peggotty went on. 'Our little Emily here –'

Mr Peggotty stopped and laughed because little Emily had run out of the room.

'My little Emily is shy,' Mr Peggotty said. 'She doesn't like people talking about her. Now, Ham, tell these young gentlemen your news.'

Ham laughed. 'I'm going to be married, sir,' he said. 'Little Emily has agreed to be my wife! I'm the luckiest man alive!'

'Congratulations, Ham!' I cried. I turned to look at Steerforth and he was smiling too.

That night, Steerforth made everyone feel happy. Even Mrs Gummidge smiled and began to look cheerful too. But little Emily was very quiet and she looked at Steerforth all the time.

It was nearly midnight when Steerforth and I left the old boat.

'Emily's a very pretty girl,' Steerforth said, as we walked back to the inn. 'That young fisherman isn't good enough for her.' I was surprised and a little upset by my friend's words.

'Ham will be a good husband for little Emily,' I said. 'They have known each other all their lives. When she was a little girl, Emily wanted to be a lady. But that's not possible, of course.'

'So little Emily wanted to be a lady,' Steerforth said slowly. 'That's a strange wish for a fisherman's daughter.'

My friend and I stayed in Yarmouth for about two weeks. Steerforth went out sailing with Ham every day. In the evenings, Steerforth often sat by the fire in the old boat, talking to his new friends. Sometimes I was there too, but I was usually with my dear Peggotty.

One evening, I returned from Blunderstone where I had been visiting my parents' graves. Steerforth was sitting alone in the old boat, staring at the fire. As he turned to look at me, his face was hard and angry.

'What's the matter?' I asked in surprise.

'I was wishing that I was a better man,' Steerforth said. 'My mother has spoilt me all my life. Sometimes I behave badly. Then I hate myself, Copperfield.'

'Then you are the only one who does!' I said, laughing. 'All these good people are now your friends. They like you and respect[49] you. And so do I.'

'Thank you, young Copperfield,' Steerforth said. 'You always cheer me up. But I'm restless, you know. I'm always looking for something different. I always want something new to interest me.'

He stood up. 'I think that I've found a new interest. It's sailing,' he said.

'Mr Peggotty tells me that you are a very good sailor,' I said. 'But you are good at so many things, Steerforth.'

'Well, we shall see,' he said. 'I've bought a boat. Mr Peggotty and Ham will paint it and make it ready to sail. They can look after it, when I am not here.'

'And you will pay them, I suppose,' I said. 'That will be a great help to them both.'

'I've given my boat a new name,' Steerforth said, smiling. 'I am going to call her the *Little Emily*. What do you think of that?'

'It is a fine idea,' I replied. 'Everyone will be delighted.'

9

My Life Changes

The next morning, I had a letter from my aunt. She had found the right career for me. She suggested that I should become a solicitor.

'What is a solicitor, Steerforth?' I asked my friend.

'A kind of lawyer,' he replied. 'Solicitors deal with civil cases[50]. For example, if there is a problem with a will[51]. Solicitors are well paid, Copperfield.'

My aunt came to London to talk to me about her idea.

'There is just one problem, aunt,' I said. 'I shall have to be articled to an experienced lawyer. That will cost a lot of money.'

'It will cost one thousand pounds and I will pay it,' Aunt Betsy replied. 'I think of you as my own son, David. You have done very well, so far, and I want you to be a success. I have arranged a meeting with a London lawyer called Mr Spenlow. I'll take you to see him this afternoon.'

Mr Spenlow was a neat, smartly dressed gentleman. Soon all the arrangements were made. I would work for him for a month. If I did well, I would become an articled clerk. Mr Spenlow would train me to be a solicitor.

My Aunt Betsy was very pleased and so was I. But she had another surprise for me.

'You must have somewhere to live,' my aunt told me. 'I think that I've found some rooms you will like. They are near the River Thames and they are not too expensive.'

I smiled. 'You think of everything, Aunt,' I said.

And so there I was in London – a young man with his own place to live in. A young man with a fine career before him! I wrote to Steerforth at once and invited him to come and see me. A few days later, he did.

'My dear Steerforth! I am delighted to see you,' I said. 'Do you like my new home? Why don't we have dinner together?'

'That's what I've come about,' Steerforth replied. 'I'm meeting two friends tonight. Why don't you join us?'

The four of us dined together and I know that I drank far too much wine.

'Let's go to the theatre!' someone said, and soon we were in the crowded street. For some reason, I found it difficult to walk and I had to hold on to Steerforth's arm.

A few minutes later, we were all in a hot, crowded theatre and I felt very ill. I found it difficult to understand what the actors were saying too. Suddenly I saw Agnes Wickfield sitting in a seat in front of me.

'My...*dear*...*Agnes*,' I called. Everyone told me to be quiet and Agnes looked very unhappy. I could not understand why.

'*Wha*...*what are you doing here*...*Agnes?*' I said. Then Steerforth pulled me to my feet.

'We must take you home, young Copperfield,' he said.

That was the last thing I remembered. When I woke up the next morning, I was very unhappy. I had been drunk and Agnes had seen me! Would she ever forgive me? Could I ever forgive myself?

Later that day, Agnes sent me a letter, asking me to meet her. She and her father were in London, on business.

As usual, my dear sister Agnes, was happy to see me. Her calm, gentle face made me feel even more unhappy.

'My dear Agnes, you are my good angel[52],' I said, smiling sadly. 'I'm so sorry that I behaved badly last night. Will you ever forgive me?'

'I've forgotten about it already,' she replied. 'But I'm worried about your friend, Steerforth. I fear that he is your *bad* angel.'

'But Steerforth is a good friend!' I cried. 'He looked after me at school and he looks after me now.'

'James Steerforth is *not* a good friend,' Agnes said quietly. 'He is a gentleman, I know. But he wastes too much money and he is wasting his life, too. Why does Steerforth spend so much time in Yarmouth? The Peggottys are simple people and they trust him. Tell them to be careful.'

I shook my head because I did not agree.

'But I want to talk to you about someone else,' Agnes went on. 'Uriah Heep – I think that we agree about *him*,' she said.

'Heep is very unpleasant and not humble at all,' I said quickly. 'Why do you want to talk about him?'

'He wants to become papa's partner,' Agnes said sadly.

'But your father must not allow that!' I cried.

'I think that papa is afraid of Uriah,' Agnes told me. 'Heep knows everything about the business now. He makes my father drink too much and then he cannot think clearly. Oh, David, I am so afraid. I do not know what to do.'

I had never seen Agnes cry before, but she began to cry now.

'Agnes, my dear sister, I'll speak to Heep,' I said.

'Please don't upset him,' Agnes said. 'If you do, you'll upset my father too. Uriah is here in London with us. He is downstairs in the office now. Speak to him as you leave, but *please* don't upset him.'

As I went downstairs, I looked into the small office.

'Oh, it's Master ... excuse me ... *Mr* Copperfield!' Heep cried, twisting his body like a snake. 'I am still *humble*,' he said, 'but I do believe that I may soon be Mr Wickfield's partner. Do you remember suggesting that, *Mr* Copperfield, many years ago?'

'I did not really believe that it would be possible,' I said.

Uriah smiled. 'No one respects Mr Wickfield now,' he replied. 'He would have lost his business long ago, if I hadn't helped him. Yes, Mr Wickfield's humble clerk has saved him from ruin!'

'I am glad to hear it,' I said coldly.

'Oh, thank you, thank you!' Uriah cried. 'And there is something else that you will be glad to hear. It is about me and Miss Agnes.'

'What do you mean?' I asked.

'I mean that, *humble* as I am, I love Miss Agnes with all my heart!' Uriah replied.

He twisted his body like a snake and I *hated* him with all *my* heart.

'Miss Agnes loves her father, of course she does,' Heep went on. 'She will do anything to help him. I hope to marry her soon. I hope that very much!'

I did not want to listen to him any longer. I walked out of the office as quickly as I could.

A few days later, Agnes and her father left London and returned to Canterbury. I went to say goodbye to them. Uriah was on the same coach. I felt very sad as I watched them drive away.

10

I Fall in Love

I was now working for Mr Spenlow and my training was going well. After several months, I became his articled clerk.

Mr Spenlow was a widower with one daughter. They lived in Norwood, a village to the south of London. Mr Spenlow was pleased with my work and he invited me to stay with him for a few days, from Saturday until Monday. I drove to Norwood with Mr Spenlow, in his carriage. After a time, we stopped outside a gate which opened into a fine garden. I followed Mr Spenlow into the house.

'Mr Copperfield, this is my daughter, Dora,' Mr Spenlow said.

Dora Spenlow was a beautiful, bright-eyed girl with fair, curly hair and a sweet smile. I took one look at her and fell deeply in love. Yes, I was in love with Dora Spenlow!

Dora had just returned from her school in Paris. She was now living with her father and her Aunt Lavinia. I was told all these things, but my thoughts were only of Dora.

There were several other guests at dinner, but I saw only Dora.

Dora spoke to me and later, she sang. Her voice was very beautiful, but I did not hear a word. I went to bed that night and dreamt of Dora.

The next morning, I got up early and went for a walk in the garden. I turned a corner and there was Dora! She was with her little dog, Jip.

'You ... you are out early, Miss Spenlow,' I said.

'It's the brightest time of day, isn't it?' Dora replied, swinging her curls.

'It is brighter now, because I have seen you, Miss Spenlow,' I said.

'You are very kind, Mr Copperfield!' Dora said, smiling sweetly.

Jip snarled at me and showed his teeth. Then he started barking as loudly as he could. The little dog was jealous of me! Dora picked the dog up and kissed him. Then *I* was jealous of *Jip*!

We walked together to a rose-garden which was full of sweetly-smelling flowers. Dora held up Jip so that he could smell the roses. She laughed and I laughed too. Jip barked. I think that we were all very happy.

My heart and mind were now full of *Dora*. I hoped that Mr Spenlow would invite me to Norwood again, but he did not.

Then one day, Mr Spenlow called me into his office.

'It is my daughter's birthday next week,' he said. 'We are driving into the country, for a picnic[53]. Perhaps you would like to come, Copperfield.'

I did no more work that day. The next morning, a little note arrived for me. It said: ***Don't forget!*** It was signed: ***Dora.***

Forget? I thought of nothing else for the rest of the week.

At last, it was the day of the picnic. It was a beautiful morning.

I got up very early and bought some flowers. I hired a smart grey horse and rode it to Norwood. When I arrived, Dora was already sitting in the garden with her best friend, Miss Julia Mills. Dora was wearing a dress as blue as the sky and a pretty little bonnet. Jip was there too, of course. He barked when I gave Dora the flowers.

'Oh, thank you, Mr Copperfield! What pretty flowers!' she said.

I rode my horse behind Mr Spenlow's little carriage. Dora sat in the carriage, with her back to the horses. We were able to look at each other all the time.

The picnic place was a soft green hill with trees at the top of it. Several other people were already there. A young man, with red hair, sat next to Dora. She smiled at him and I was very jealous. Then I smiled at a girl in a pink dress and that made Dora jealous too. For about an hour, we refused to look at each other. Miss Mills told us not to be silly and so I kissed Dora's hand. Later, Dora held my arm as we walked under the trees.

On the way home, Mr Spenlow fell asleep. I rode beside the carriage and whispered to Dora.

When we reached Norwood again, Miss Mills spoke to me very quietly. 'Mr Copperfield,' she said. 'Dora is going to stay with me for a few days. Please call and see us.'

Of course I went. And of course I fell more deeply in love. I wanted to tell Dora my feelings, but I could not.

Then one day, Dora and I were together in Miss Mills' sitting-room. Dora held out her arms to pick up Jip, but I leaned forward quickly and held Dora in *my* arms. I told her how much I loved her. I told her that if we could not be together, I would die.

Dora began to cry and Jip began to bark. I went on talking. The more I said, the more Jip barked.

At last, we were all quiet. I was sitting next to Dora on the couch. Jip was in her arms. We were all happy, even Jip. Dora and I were now engaged to be married!

Miss Mills ran into the room and we told her everything. But we agreed that, for the moment, we would not tell Dora's father.

I sent letters to Miss Mills and she gave them to Dora. And Dora wrote to me every day. What a happy time that was! I shall never forget it.

I had not heard from Steerforth for some time, but I did not worry.

'Steerforth always does what he likes,' I thought. 'He'll walk in one evening and I'll tell him all about Dora.'

Then I had a letter from Peggotty. Her husband, old Mr Barkis, had died. I asked Mr Spenlow for a few days' holiday and I went to Yarmouth.

After the funeral, I went to Blunderstone with Peggotty. I wanted to see my parents' graves again. Peggotty told me that Ham and little Emily were to be married in two weeks' time. I was delighted.

Dora and I were now engaged to be married!

Emily was staying with some friends in Yarmouth. We were all going to meet at Mr Peggotty's boat that evening.

I must now make myself write about that terrible time. Even after all these years, I still remember exactly what happened.

It was a dark night and the wind was blowing strongly. As I went towards the old boat, I could see a light shining in the window. I hurried towards it and I was soon inside. Mr Peggotty was there, as well as my Peggotty, and Mrs Gummidge too.

'Hello, Master Davy, sir,' Mr Peggotty said. 'The others will be here soon. We have put a candle in the window and its light will guide little Emily home. She loves to see that light and know that I am here.'

A few minutes later the door opened and Ham came in.

'Where's little Emily?' his uncle asked. Ham did not answer him, but he spoke to me.

'Can you come outside, Master Davy?' Ham said. 'We want to show you something.'

I went outside with him, but little Emily was not there. I looked at Ham's pale face. 'Ham, what's the matter?' I asked.

'She's gone,' Ham replied. 'Emily has run away. And she's not alone, sir. *He* has taken her and he will ruin her! How can I tell my uncle? Read her letter, Master Davy.'

As I took the letter, the door opened and Mr Peggotty saw us standing there. Ham and I went inside the house. The women began to cry as I read the letter aloud.

> *When you, who love me, read this, I shall be far away. I shall never come back, unless he makes me a lady. That is his promise and I believe him. I am doing wrong and I know it. But he is too strong for me and I love him. Dear Ham, forget me. Dear Uncle, forgive me. Forgive your loving Emily.*

Mr Peggotty looked slowly round the room.

'Who's the man?' he said. 'I want to know his name.'

'His name is Steerforth and he's a damned villain[54]!' Ham replied.

I sat down and covered my face with my hands.

'It's not your fault[55], Master Davy,' Ham said quickly. 'He deceived[56] us all.'

I remembered that Agnes had called Steerforth my 'bad angel'. I had laughed at her, then. Dear Agnes – she was never wrong.

'I shall never forgive myself for bringing him here,' I said quietly.

Mr Peggotty put on his coat and hat.

'Where are you going?' Mrs Gummidge asked.

'I'm going to look for Emily,' he said. 'Wherever he has taken my girl, I shall find her and bring her back. Put a lighted candle in the window every night. If little Emily comes back alone, she will see it. She will know that this is still her home. Tell her that I love her and welcome her back.'

11

Some Old Friends Turn Up Again

I wrote Agnes a long letter, telling her that Dora and I were engaged. I also told her about poor little Emily and how unhappy I was about Steerforth. I knew that Agnes would understand. She replied at once in her kind way.

Peggotty was now staying with me, in London. I was helping her with her late husband's will.

One evening, Peggotty spoke to me as soon as I got home.

'A nice young man called to see you, Davy,' she said. 'His name is Thomas Traddles. He'll come back later.'

And so he did and I was delighted to see him.

'My dear Traddles,' I said. 'You look exactly as you did at school! How are you and how did you find me here?'

'Well, I'm in the law business too,' Traddles said. 'I'm training to be a barrister. One day, I heard someone talking about you. So I found out where you lived and here I am! Mrs Barkis has already told me all about you. And about your lovely Dora, of course.'

I laughed. 'What about *you*, Traddles?' I asked. 'Do you have a Dora of your own?'

'Well, yes, I do,' Traddles said, 'but her name is Sophy. We have no money, so we won't be married for years. She lives with her family in the country and I live in a very small room, here in London. I'm staying with a family called Micawber. They have even less money than I do.'

'Micawber?!' I cried. 'Is Mr Micawber a bald-headed man, with a walking stick and an eye-glass? Does he have a wife and four children?'

'That's Mr Wilkins Micawber!' Traddles said, laughing. 'He's always in debt.'

'And he's always waiting for something to turn up!' I said. 'The family was very kind to me when I was a child. I should like to see them again.'

'Then I'll come here tomorrow and I'll take you to the Micawbers myself,' Traddles said.

Mr Micawber had not changed at all. At first, he did not recognize me. When he did, he shook my hand and called to Mrs Micawber.

'My dear young friend!' he said to me. 'Do you remember the time we spent together in London and in Canterbury? Mrs

Micawber, the family and I have been living in the great city of London for a time. London is an expensive place, as you know. I've had some problems with money. But I hope, every day, that something will turn up!'

Mrs Micawber began to cry. 'I will never leave Mr Micawber!' she said. 'I never have and I never will!'

I called to the eldest child and gave him some money. Then I spoke to Traddles. The two of them went out and, very soon, they came back with food and drink for us all. We spent a pleasant evening together and Mr Micawber made a speech about me. I felt much more cheerful as I walked back to my rooms.

Thomas Traddles was not my only visitor that week.

Peggotty and I had been out shopping. As we walked up the stairs to my rooms, I saw that the sitting-room door was open. I went in quickly. To my surprise, my Aunt Betsy was sitting there! She was wearing her best shawl and holding her old cat in her arms. There were bags and boxes all round her.

'My dear aunt!' I cried, as I kissed her. 'I am glad to see you! Why didn't you tell me that you were coming?'

Peggotty was standing behind me and I took her hand.

'Aunt, this is my dear Peggotty – or Mrs Barkis, I should say.'

'How are you, Mrs Barkis?' my aunt said. 'I was sorry to hear about the death of your husband.'

'Thank you, ma'am,' Peggotty replied. She looked a little afraid of my aunt.

'David, my dear, I've got bad news,' Aunt Betsy said. 'I've lost everything. I invested[57] my money badly and I lost it. All I have is in this room. I am ruined, my dear!'

'I am very sorry to hear it,' I said quickly. 'You must stay here, of course. You looked after me when I had nothing. Now I will look after *you*. I'll do everything that I can to help you.'

'And I'll get some tea,' Peggotty said.

Soon I was telling Aunt Betsy about Dora.

My aunt shook her head sadly. 'So you think that you are in love, David,' she said.

'I *know* that I love Dora,' I replied. 'I love her with all my heart.'

'She's very pretty, I suppose?' my aunt asked.

'She's beautiful!' I said. 'My Dora is the most beautiful girl in the world! She has the prettiest curly hair and the sweetest smile that I have ever seen.'

My aunt turned her head away. 'I remember your father saying the same about your dear, silly mother,' she said quietly.

'Dora isn't silly,' I said quickly. 'She is very young and so am I. But we love each other.'

My aunt smiled sadly. 'Young and blind,' she whispered.

I began to think about myself. *I* was poor now, too. How could I stay engaged to Dora ? Then I remembered the one thousand pounds that my aunt had given to Dora's father. I spoke to Mr Spenlow the next day.

'My aunt, Miss Trotwood, has lost all her money and I want to help her,' I said. 'She gave you one thousand pounds when I was articled to you. If I stop working for you, Mr Spenlow, could you return the money?'

Mr Spenlow looked very surprised. 'I am afraid that is impossible, Mr Copperfield,' he said. 'We have a legal agreement. It cannot be changed. That is the law. You must go on working for me. I shall forget this conversation.'

When I told my friend, Traddles, he understood my problem at once.

'You have a job, Copperfield,' Traddles said. 'But you need more ways of making money. Don't worry, I know them all!

'Lawyers always want their legal documents copied,' he told

me. 'You can do that to get money now. But you should also learn to write shorthand.'

'Shorthand?' I asked, 'What's that?'

'It's a quick way of writing,' Traddles told me. 'Reporters use shorthand. They listen to Parliamentary debates[58] and write down every word of the speeches. The debates take place in the evenings and the reporters are well paid. Why don't you think about it, Copperfield?'

'I will!' I cried. 'I usually leave Mr Spenlow's office at four o'clock. I'll start learning shorthand at once!' And so I did.

Dora wrote to me. She said that she was staying at Miss Mills' house for a few days. Of course, I went to see Dora. She was more beautiful than ever. I could not lose her now!

I explained everything that had happened. 'My dearest, can you still love me, now that I am almost a beggar?' I said sadly.

'Don't be so silly, David!' Dora exclaimed. 'You're not a beggar. I'll tell Jip to bite you for telling such lies!'

'But my dearest, I am earning very little money. We must be practical,' I replied.

Dora put her hands over her ears and shook her pretty head.

'Oh, no, not practical!' she said. 'You know that I could never be practical!'

Well, I did know it, but I could not stop loving her.

My aunt wrote to Agnes and told her the bad news. In her reply, Agnes said that she would come to London to see my aunt. A few days later, my dear 'sister' Agnes, came to my rooms.

'Agnes! I'm so glad you are here. I wanted to see you more than anyone else!' I told her.

'More than Dora?' she said and smiled.

I smiled too. 'Well, not more than Dora,' I replied.

'I'm not in London alone,' Agnes went on. 'My father is with me, and Uriah Heep too. They are partners, as you know.'

She sighed and then went on. 'Uriah and his mother live in our house now,' Agnes said. 'We can never get away from them. I'm afraid that Uriah is planning something bad. I don't trust him.'

'You are quite right,' my aunt said. 'Never trust Uriah Heep. But don't let us talk about *him*.'

So we talked about our time together in Canterbury. Then Peggotty told Agnes and Aunt Betsy about my mother. Later, I told everyone how much I loved Dora. As we talked, all our troubles were forgotten, for a time. Later, when I walked with Agnes back to her inn, she looked a little happier.

'Dear sister,' I said, before I left her, 'remember that my aunt and I will always be your friends. Send for us if you need help. Look after your father and do not trust Heep.'

'Thank you, David, I will do as you say,' Agnes answered quietly. 'And I hope all goes well with you and Dora.'

Soon after this, Peggotty went back to her house in Yarmouth. She and my aunt were good friends now. Aunt Betsy and I were both sorry to say goodbye to her.

A few days later, Mr Spenlow called me into his office. When he saw me, he frowned.

'You have been deceiving me, Mr Copperfield,' he said. 'I have found out that you have been meeting my daughter in secret. You've been writing letters to her too. Dora is my only child and I want her to marry well. You are not to see her again. You must not write her any more letters. Do you understand?'

'Mr Spenlow, I love your daughter!' I said. 'Dora loves me too! We are engaged!'

'You are *not* engaged to my daughter, Mr Copperfield and you never will be,' Mr Spenlow replied.

'I know that we are both very young,' I began, 'but time will change that. I have little money at the moment. But I am working hard to change that too. I –'

'Please don't say any more,' Mr Spenlow said. 'I have made up my mind. You must forget my daughter. That is all, Mr Copperfield.'

'But Mr Spenlow,' I said. 'How did you – ?'

'How did I find out about you and Dora?' he said. 'Well, Dora's dog found one of your letters. He was playing with it when my sister Lavinia saw him.'

I was very, very unhappy. I told my aunt everything when I got home and I did not sleep all night.

The next morning, I went to Mr Spenlow's office, but he was not there.

'There is terrible news, Copperfield – terrible news about Mr Spenlow,' his clerk said.

'What has happened?' I asked.

'He's dead!'

'Mr Spenlow is dead? How? When?' I cried.

'He dined in London last night and then drove down to Norwood by himself, as usual. But when his little carriage got home, he was not in it. His servants found him a mile away. He was lying on the road – dead.'

I could not write to Dora, but I wrote to her friend, Miss Mills.

Miss Mills told me that my little Dora was crying all day. And she said the same words again and again. 'Oh, poor Papa! Poor Papa!'

12

Uriah Heep

My aunt was now very worried about me and my unhappiness about Dora.

'Why don't you go to Canterbury for a few days?' Aunt Betsy said. 'I would like to hear how the Wickfields are.'

I had very little work to do at the office, so I agreed.

After the noise and crowds of London, the old city of Canterbury was very peaceful.

I walked to Mr Wickfield's house and there I had a great surprise. Mr Micawber was sitting in Uriah Heep's old office, working busily.

'Mr Micawber! What are *you* doing here?' I cried.

'My dear Copperfield,' Micawber replied, putting down his pen. 'As you see, I am now a clerk in the offices of Wickfield and Heep. I am enjoying the work and my friend Heep has been very good to me. The Micawber family now lives in Heep's old house. And Heep himself has been kind enough to give me some help with … '

'Has he lent you money?' I asked.

Mr Micawber smiled. 'Heep is my good friend,' he said. 'Heep has been very helpful to me, very helpful. Shall I take you to see him?'

'Thank you, I know the way,' I said. 'I have come to see Miss Wickfield, not Heep.'

Agnes was sitting alone in a little room, upstairs. She welcomed me with a sweet smile.

'My dear sister!' I cried. 'Whenever I see you, my troubles seem further away. I rely on[59] you, just as I always did.'

'But you have Dora now,' Agnes said quietly.

'Of course,' I said quickly. 'But *she* relies on *me*. My Dora is easily upset and she needs me now, more than ever. But I don't know what to do. I have come for your advice, Agnes.'

'Then there must be no more secrets,' Agnes said, when I told her everything. 'Write to Dora's Aunt Lavinia. Ask her if you can visit Dora sometimes. Tell Aunt Lavinia the truth. Tell her how much you love Dora. She will understand, I am sure.'

'Agnes, you are right, as usual,' I said. 'Thank you, dear sister.'

The Heeps now lived in the Wickfields' house, but there was still a room there for me.

Mr Wickfield himself looked much older, but Uriah and his mother had not changed at all. They made sure that I was never alone with Mr Wickfield, or Agnes, at any time.

Early the next evening, I decided to go for a walk. I wanted to be by myself. I had not gone far, when I heard a voice calling my name. It was Uriah Heep.

'You walk very fast, Mr Copperfield!' he said. 'Wait for me! Let's walk together.'

'I was hoping to be alone for a time,' I said.

Uriah smiled in his unpleasant way. 'Mother and I are very *humble*,' he said. 'But some people aren't, Mr Copperfield. You don't want to speak to me, because I am *humble*. But I have something to say to *you*. As you know, I love my Agnes with all my heart. But Mother thinks that *you* love my Agnes too.'

'Then tell Mrs Heep that I think of Miss Wickfield as a sister,' I replied. 'I am engaged to another young lady.'

'Thank you. That makes me feel very *humble*,' said Uriah, twisting his hands together. 'My late father taught me to be *humble*. I have been *humble* all my life.

'But now I've got a little power,' he went on. 'And I will use that power, Mr Copperfield. Oh yes, I will use that power!'

At dinner that night, Uriah was very cheerful. When Agnes and Mrs Heep went into the sitting-room, Uriah filled Mr Wickfield's wine-glass several times.

'Let us drink to your daughter,' said Uriah, smiling terribly. He lifted his own glass. 'To Agnes Wickfield!' he said. 'I am a *humble* man, Mr Wickfield. But one day soon, your Agnes will be my wife!'

When he heard these words, Mr Wickfield gave a terrible cry. He stood up, knocked over his glass of wine and began to shout. 'No! No!'

'I hope that you have not gone mad, Mr Wickfield,' Heep said calmly. 'I am your business partner. Why can't I be your son-in-law too?'

I put my arm round Mr Wickfield's shoulders and tried to calm him.

'Look at that man!' Mr Wickfield cried. 'He has ruined me! He has taken everything I have, except my dear Agnes. And now he wants her!'

'I have saved your business for you,' Uriah said coldly. 'But I could do you harm and you know it. You have drunk too much wine. Be careful what you say!'

Mr Wickfield sat down again and began to cry. 'It is all my fault,' he whispered. 'I have been weak and foolish. I love my daughter but now I have lost her. Oh, Agnes, forgive me!'

At that moment the door opened and Agnes came in.

'Papa, you are not well,' she said. 'Let me take you to bed.'

'He didn't know what he was saying,' Uriah said. 'We'll be friends again in the morning.'

I went upstairs too. I opened a book and tried to read. Just before midnight, Agnes came quietly into the room and spoke to me.

'You will be going early tomorrow, so I'll say goodbye to you now,' she said.

She was smiling, but her face was very pale. I knew that she had been crying.

'Dear Agnes! Is there nothing that I can do?' I asked. 'Your loving heart is too good to be given away to Heep. You are more than a sister to me, Agnes. You know how much I love you. Your love would be a great gift to any man. Do not give it to *him*.'

Agnes looked at me. Her eyes were full of love. Then she smiled. 'I shall never marry Uriah Heep,' she said. 'My dear brother, go back to your Dora.' Then she quickly left the room.

As I got onto the coach the next morning, Uriah Heep was there to say goodbye.

'Everything is all right now,' he said. 'I am a *humble* man, Copperfield, so it's easy for me to say sorry. I spoke too soon, that is all. My time will come, Copperfield. My time will come!'

As he spoke, he held my hand and smiled wickedly. 'Let's say goodbye as friends,' he said.

I was so angry that I pulled my hand away and raised it to hit him.

Uriah Heep moved away quickly. 'Take care, Copperfield! Take care!' he whispered. 'I forgive you, my friend. But you tried to hit me, Copperfield, and I won't forget that.'

When I got back to London, I told my aunt everything that had happened. She looked very unhappy and shook her head several times. Then I told her about the advice that Agnes had given me.

'Agnes thinks that I should write to Dora's aunt and tell her my feelings,' I said. 'Then, perhaps I shall be allowed to visit Dora. After that, who knows what will happen?'

My aunt shook her head again. 'Blind, so blind,' she whispered, but I did not understand her.

Before I went to bed, I wrote to Dora's Aunt Lavinia.

13

I Am Married

Time went by and soon I was twenty-one. What had I done with my life so far?

I was now a reporter of Parliamentary debates and my reports were printed in the morning papers.

I had started to write my own words too – I was an author. I wrote short stories for magazines and they were published.

I moved into a little house in north London and my aunt came to live near me. And what did all this mean? Yes! Dora and I were going to be married!

My Aunt Betsy and Dora's Aunt Lavinia were now good friends. My Dora needed new clothes for the wedding. Aunt Lavinia helped Dora buy them. Both the aunts found furniture for our new home – the home where Dora and I were going to live.

Peggotty came to London too. She cleaned every piece of furniture until it shone.

And then, at last, it was our wedding day. Traddles was at the church with his Sophy. Agnes came from Canterbury. The two aunts were there, and my dear Peggotty too. I was married to my dearest Dora and I could not believe it.

Later, Dora and I drove away together and we took Jip with us.

'Are you happy, now?' Dora whispered to me.

'I am very happy, my dearest,' I said.

So Dora and I were living in our own little house at last. It was strange and very delightful to have my dear Dora always near me. We would be happy for the rest of our lives!

When I sat writing in the evenings, Dora was sitting

opposite me. When I worked late in Parliament, Dora waited for me at home. I found it all difficult to believe, but I was very happy.

However, we did have a problem. Neither Dora nor I knew anything about housekeeping.

We had one servant – Mary Anne – but she was no help at all. In fact, I think that Dora was a little afraid of her.

One evening, we sat waiting for dinner, but it never came. At last, I spoke to Dora.

'What has happened to our dinner?' I said. 'It should have been ready an hour ago. Why don't you ask Mary Anne about it, Dora?'

'Oh, no, I couldn't do that!' Dora cried. 'Let's not talk about her, Davy. It makes me so unhappy!'

'It makes me a little unhappy to have no dinner!' I said. 'We really must talk about this, Dora.'

'Oh, now you're going to be cross!' Dora said and there were tears in her eyes.

'No, I'm not cross,' I said. 'But dinner was late yesterday too. And the day before, it wasn't cooked properly.'

Dora turned her head away from me and began to cry.

'You are telling me that I am a bad wife!' she said. 'You are sorry that you married me! You are cruel, Davy!'

'My dearest Dora, I love you. You know I do. But things are very uncomfortable, you know. What happened to that cookery book I bought for you?'

Dora went on crying and she shook her head sadly.

'I could not understand it,' she said. 'I have never cooked in my life. How can I start now?'

I sighed. 'Dora is right,' I thought. 'Housekeeping must be difficult for her.'

I had to go out again that evening. When I returned, my aunt was sitting by the fire, waiting for me.

'Is anything the matter, Aunt?' I said. 'Where's Dora?'

'She was a little upset, so she went to bed,' my aunt said.

'I'm afraid that I upset Dora,' I replied. 'I was only trying to help her.'

My aunt smiled sadly and shook her head. 'Our Dora is like a flower that cannot live in a strong, cold wind. You mustn't be that wind, David. Dora is a loving and delightful child. She will never change. Remember what happened to your mother. The Murdstones tried to make *her* change, but she couldn't. Neither can Dora.'

'Then perhaps you can advise her, Aunt,' I said. 'You will know the right things to say.'

'No, David,' my aunt replied. 'I am not going to say anything. That would be quite wrong. You must decide how to live your own lives. That is marriage, my dear.'

In the morning, Dora and I were friends again. Things went wrong again, of course. We hired a new servant, but she was worse than Mary Anne. There was either too much food or too little. We were spending a lot of money too. It was money that we did not have. But I remembered my aunt's words and I was very gentle with my dear wife. I loved her and that was enough.

One evening, I invited Traddles to dinner. Dora was delighted and I hoped that all would go well.

'My love, what have you got in that dish?' I asked as we sat down at the table.

'Fish, my dear,' Dora whispered.

But the fish smelt bad and we could not eat it. Dora's eyes filled with tears.

'Don't worry,' I said. 'Tell the servant to bring in the meat.'

But most of the meat was under-cooked. We ate what we could, with plenty of potatoes. We drank a glass or two of wine. Then Dora made us some tea and afterwards, she sang to us. The evening had started badly, but ended very pleasantly.

When Traddles had left, Dora kissed me. 'Thank you for not being cross,' she said. 'You must teach me to be a good wife, Davy. I shall try very hard to learn!'

'I shall have to learn to cook first,' I said and laughed.

'I'm sure that Agnes can cook,' Dora said sadly. 'She does everything so well.'

'Agnes has looked after her father for many years,' I said. 'Your life has been very different.'

'Yes, I am your child-wife, Davy. Will you call me that? Then, when I do something silly you can think – *it's only my child-wife*. But your child-wife loves you, never forget that!'

Dora did try much harder after that. I sometimes saw her looking at the pictures in the cookery book. She also tried to do the housekeeping accounts[60]. She wrote down the amount of money we spent in a very big book. Then she tried to add up the figures. But she never got the right answer.

I was writing more stories now and people enjoyed reading them. Dora tried to keep Jip quiet when I was writing, but he always wanted to bark and play. Then I would put down my pen and smile. The little dog and my dear Dora looked so happy together.

So time went by, and soon Dora and I had been married for a year and a half. I loved Dora. I had always loved her. But now I knew that there was something missing in our marriage. We were not equal partners. When I tried to teach Dora to be practical, I made her unhappy. At last, I accepted that Dora – my child-wife – could never change. *I* had to change, not Dora.

And so the second year of our marriage began. Then Dora told me that we were expecting a child. Our baby was born, but it lived for only a few days. After that sad time, Dora was never well.

'I'll be better soon,' I heard Dora say to my aunt one day. 'Then I shall make Jip run about with me, as we used to do.'

'I'm afraid that Jip is getting older, like the rest of us,' my aunt replied with a smile.

'Poor Jip getting old? I don't want to think about it,' Dora said. 'We'll soon be running about again, Jip and I, won't we, Jip?'

But day after day, Dora lay on the couch with Jip by her side. I carried her downstairs every morning and upstairs again at night. We laughed about it, but every day Dora felt lighter in my arms. Every evening, I sat downstairs alone and tried to write.

Aunt Betsy had called Dora a flower.

'A flower is beautiful, but it has a very short life,' I thought. I began to be afraid that my Dora's life would be short too.

14

Little Emily Comes Home

Although so much had happened in my own life, I had not forgotten Mr Peggotty.

As he had promised, he was looking for his niece, little Emily. My friend, James Steerforth had taken her away, 'to be a lady'. But we all knew that one day, he would be tired of her. Then she would need her family again.

I saw Mr Peggotty once, before I was married. He had not found his niece, but he was able to give me some news of her.

The old fisherman was waiting outside my rooms, when I returned home, one winter evening. His hair was long and it had become grey. But he looked strong and his eyes were clear and bright.

When we were sitting down together, Mr Peggotty told me his story.

'I guessed that he – that man – had taken my Emily out of England,' Mr Peggotty said. 'So I went across the sea to France. I walked and walked. I asked people as I went along, but there was no news of her. So I came back to England.'

'How long ago?' I asked.

'Four days,' he replied. 'I went home to Yarmouth. The candle was shining in the window of the old boat and Mrs Gummidge was sitting there, alone. She showed me some letters. They were from little Emily and she was asking me for forgiveness.'

'Did Emily say where she was?' I asked.

'This last letter has a name written on it,' Mr Peggotty replied. 'But Emily was leaving the next day. Here's the letter. Have you heard of the place, Master Davy?'

'It's a town on the River Rhine,' I said.

'Then I can find it,' said Mr Peggotty. 'I'll ask about little Emily there. Someone may remember her.'

'How is Ham?' I asked quietly.

'He works hard – day and night,' Mr Peggotty replied. 'Where there is danger, he is there. But he still loves little Emily. He always will. I must go now, sir.'

I shook hands with Mr Peggotty and he left me. I was very sad as I watched him walk away.

I did not see Mr Peggotty again for more than two years. Dora was ill and Aunt Betsy was often in our house, looking after her.

One day, early in the morning, my aunt and I were walking in the garden. I looked up and saw Mr Peggotty standing at the gate. I ran towards him and shook his hand.

'Do you have any news?' I asked, and he smiled.

'Yes, thank God, Master Davy,' he said. 'I think that my little Emily has come back to England.'

'How do you know?' I asked.

'She wrote to me,' he replied. 'I think that you can help me find her.'

'I'll do everything that I can,' I said.

We all sat down together and Mr Peggotty told us his news.

'I went to France. I went to Switzerland. I searched for my Emily for many weeks. The weeks turned into months, but I went on looking for my girl. I walked along many roads and stayed in many strange places. Sometimes I got news of Emily and that man, but I never found them.

'Then I wanted to see the sea again, so I got on a ship that was sailing to southern Italy – to the port of Naples. I was told that many rich Englishmen had houses outside the city and near the sea. I went from house to house, talking to the servants. At last, I had news of my little Emily.'

My aunt smiled. 'So you saw her?' she said. 'But what did you say to *him*?'

Mr Peggotty shook his head.

'They had both left Naples,' he said. 'I spoke to their housekeeper. She told me that Steerforth had become tired of little Emily. He had given her to his servant.'

'What do you mean?' I cried.

'Steerforth's plan was that my little Emily should marry his servant,' Mr Peggotty replied.

'Poor little Emily, poor child,' my aunt said quietly. 'What did she do?'

'The housekeeper told me that little Emily screamed and cried. Steerforth's servant locked Emily in her room. But she climbed out of the window and disappeared. People thought that she had drowned herself. The servant left soon afterwards.'

'What *had* happened to little Emily? How do you know that she is alive?' my aunt asked Mr Peggotty. He smiled.

'My little Emily had made friends with some fishermen and their families,' he said. 'She often played with their children on the beach, by the sea.'

I remembered how little Emily and I used to play together on the beach at Yarmouth. I remembered the time when we had walked by the sea, near her old home.

'Those good people helped her to find a boat which was going to France,' Mr Peggotty went on. 'Little Emily wrote to me from there. She told me that she was working as a lady's servant. Then I had no news for some time. But I guessed that she would go to London.'

'London is a very big place,' my aunt said sadly.

Mr Peggotty smiled. 'I've heard from little Emily again,' he said. 'Here's the letter. She sent it to Yarmouth and there's an address. Look at it and tell me where the place is, Master Davy.'

I was able to tell him at once. The address was in a poor part of London. I was worried about little Emily, but I said nothing.

'Then I'll be off again,' Mr Peggotty said. 'When I have found little Emily, I'll come back and tell you.'

I hoped with all my heart that he would find her.

I did not see Mr Peggotty for nearly a month. Then he came to my house again and told me the next part of his sad story.

'Well, I found her, Master Davy,' he began. 'And oh, the poor child had changed! All her money had gone and she looked very ill. When I called her my dear child, she knelt down and held my hands in hers. "Oh, Uncle!" she cried. "I've seen your dear face in my dreams again and again. There has never been a minute when I did not think of you and my home! Can you ever forgive me?"

'I pulled my little Emily up and kissed her,' Mr Peggotty went on. 'I told her that I would never let her go again.'

'Are you taking her back to Yarmouth?' I asked.

Mr Peggotty shook his head. 'She doesn't want to go there,' he said. 'I have another plan. I'm taking little Emily with me to another country, far away. We are emigrating[61] to Australia. We can both begin a new life. No one will know about little Emily there.'

'What about Ham?' I asked.

'My sister is living in Ham's house now and she looks after him. Mrs Gummidge is with them too,' Mr Peggotty said. 'I am going back to Yarmouth to say goodbye. Would you come with me, Master Davy? That would make things easier for me. Little Emily is in a safe place now. Nothing and no one will harm her.'

I spoke to Dora and she was happy for me to go. Next morning, Mr Peggotty and I were on the Yarmouth coach.

It was strange to meet all my old friends again. Mr Peggotty went to the old boat to pack his things and Mrs Gummidge went with him. Later, I spoke to Ham as we walked together on the beach. Ham spoke first.

'Have you seen her, Master Davy?' he asked quietly, looking at the sea.

I shook my head. 'No. It would upset her too much,' I said sadly. 'But if you have a message for her, I'll write to her.'

'Tell her that I loved her,' Ham said. 'I still do, Master Davy. Tell her I remember the happy times. I'll never forget her and I'll never marry now. I wish her well in her new life. My uncle will look after her, I am sure of that. I am losing both of them, I know. But it is the best thing to do. Give my uncle my thanks. I know that you are going back to the house, so I'll leave you now. And thank you, sir, for coming with him. Goodbye.'

I watched the young fisherman as he walked away across the beach. Then I turned towards the old boat.

The old place looked very strange in the moonlight. My dear friends were leaving their home for the last time and the boat would soon be empty.

As I went inside for the last time, I felt very sad.

'Come, Mrs Gummidge,' Mr Peggotty was saying kindly. 'It's time to go. I'll take you and your things to Ham's house.'

Suddenly, Mrs Gummidge began to cry. 'Please, Mr Peggotty, take me with you to Australia!' she said. 'I'll look after you and little Emily, just as I have always done.'

Mr Peggotty was very surprised. 'But it's a long way to Australia and it's a long, hard journey,' he said. 'And it will be a hard life when we get there.'

'I know,' Mrs Gummidge replied. ' I don't care. I want to go with you. Please say that I can.'

Mr Peggotty smiled. He carried out Mrs Gummidge's box, blew out the candle and locked the door for the last time.

The next morning, the three of us were on the coach to London.

15

That Villain Heep!

A few weeks later, I received a surprising letter from Mr Micawber. He wrote from Canterbury, where he was working for Wickfield and Heep. He wanted to meet me in London. He gave me the place and the time. And he asked me to bring Thomas Traddles with me.

Mr Micawber gave no reason for the meeting, but he was very unhappy about something. I went to see Traddles. When I showed him the letter, he laughed and shook his head.

'What can Mr Micawber mean?' Traddles asked. 'He writes about villainy, but whose villainy? And he writes about fraud[62]. What does he mean?

'Now I have a letter to show *you*, Copperfield,' Traddles went on. 'It is from *Mrs* Micawber! She is very worried about her husband. He has been behaving very strangely. She is afraid that he is going mad!'

'We must find out what is wrong, Traddles,' I said. 'I'll reply to Mr Micawber at once. We must meet him, of course.'

We all met three days later. As soon as he saw us, Mr Micawber started to cry. At first, he was too upset to tell us anything.

'Come back with us to my aunt's house, Mr Micawber,' I said. 'We can talk about your problem there. My wife, Dora, is not well and I do not want to upset her. But my aunt will be delighted to meet you. She knows how kind you were to me in the past.'

As I expected, my aunt welcomed Mr Micawber warmly. 'You and your wife were kind to my nephew when he was a boy,' she said. 'I shall always be grateful to you. How can he help you now?'

Mr Micawber took out his handkerchief and began to cry again.

'Mr Micawber,' I said. 'What is the matter? Please tell us. We are all your friends.'

'What is the matter?' Mr Micawber repeated. 'Villainy, deceit and fraud are the matter! I am speaking about that villain HEEP!'

'What do you mean, Mr Micawber?' Traddles asked. 'Tell us everything you know about Heep. What do you want us to do?'

'I want the world to know about that villain HEEP! I want Miss Wickfield to know the deceit of that wicked man HEEP! I want you, Miss Wickfield's friends, to help me. We must bring HEEP to justice[63]!' Mr Micawber cried.

'Can you prove[64] that Heep is a villain?' Traddles asked. 'None of us likes Heep, but you must give us proof. Can you do that?'

'I CAN and I WILL!' Mr Micawber cried. 'Come down to Canterbury and Wilkins Micawber will tell you everything! We will show HEEP that we know the truth!'

So my aunt, Traddles and myself agreed to meet Mr Micawber in Mr Wickfield's office in Canterbury. In front of us all, Mr Micawber would tell Heep what he knew.

My aunt did not want to leave Dora, but Dora laughed.

'I am not really ill,' she said. 'You know that. I'm just a little tired sometimes. I shall stay in bed and rest. If you don't go to Canterbury, I'll make Jip bark at you all day!'

We travelled to Canterbury that same evening. There Mr Micawber told us everything he knew. The next day, Mr Micawber went to his office at the usual time. Five minutes later, my aunt, Traddles and myself all walked into Mr Wickfield's house.

'Good morning, Mr Micawber,' I said. 'Is Miss Wickfield at home?'

'Mr Wickfield is ill, sir,' Mr Micawber replied. 'But Miss Wickfield will be happy to see old friends.' He was speaking very calmly now. 'Let me take you to Mr Wickfield's office,' he said.

Uriah Heep was sitting in the office alone. When he saw us, he frowned. Then he stood up and shook my hand.

'This is a pleasant surprise,' he said, with his usual smile. 'Ah! And here is Miss Trotwood too. Things have changed since you were last here.'

'But I see that *you* have not changed at all,' my aunt replied, as she sat down.

'You are not busy, Mr Heep?' Traddles asked.

'Not at the moment. But, of course, I have to do all the work now. My partner, Mr Wickfield is too ill to help me.'

Heep turned to his clerk. 'Micawber, fetch Miss Wickfield,' he said. 'And tell my mother that we have visitors. *She* will be happy to see old friends again!'

When Agnes came into the room, she looked pale, but very calm. While Uriah was smiling at her, Traddles went out quietly.

'You can go now, Micawber,' Heep said, but his clerk did not move. 'What are you waiting for?' Uriah said, more loudly. 'Why don't you obey me?'

'Because I don't want to!' Mr Micawber replied.

Heep's face went white with anger. 'Get out, you villain!' he said. 'I'll speak to you later.'

'If there is a villain in this room, that villain's name is HEEP!' Mr Micawber cried.

Heep was not smiling now. He looked hard at us all and frowned. 'I see. You have planned this,' he said. 'You, Copperfield, have always hated me. And now you bring your friends here to speak against me! Take care, Copperfield! And you, Miss Wickfield – take care – or I'll ruin your father, as well as Micawber.'

Heep looked quickly round the room. 'Where's your other friend? And where's mother?' he shouted.

'Mrs Heep is here,' Traddles said, coming back into the room.

Uriah Heep turned to Traddles and snarled like a dog. 'Who *are* you and what are you doing here?' he said.

'I am a barrister and a friend of Mr Wickfield,' Traddles replied. 'I have his permission to act for[65] him.'

'The old fool's always drunk!' Heep said angrily. 'He doesn't know what he's doing. *I* act for him, not you! You got his permission by fraud.'

'There *has* been fraud,' Traddles said. 'But *you* have broken the law, not me. Your clerk, Mr Micawber, has told us everything.'

Mrs Heep looked from one face to another. 'My Uriah,' she began, 'remember to be humble —'

'Be quiet, mother!' Heep said quickly.

'But my Uriah —'

'Be quiet mother!' Heep snarled again. 'Let me speak to them!'

Uriah Heep no longer looked humble. He looked very angry and very wicked indeed.

'Copperfield, you surprise me,' he said. 'You call yourself a gentleman, but you have very strange friends. As you know, *I've* always been a humble clerk. Now, Micawber,' Heep went on. 'Let's hear from *you*.'

Mr Micawber smiled as he picked up a large piece of paper and began to read.

'I am a clerk in the office of Wickfield and Heep,' he said. 'At first, I thought that Heep was my friend. He lent me money. But then he used me to deceive Mr Wickfield. We lied to him. We told Mr Wickfield that he had lost all his money. But it was a lie. That money had been taken by Heep himself.

'Many people had given Mr Wickfield money to invest,' Mr Micawber went on. 'Heep had taken their money too. Mr Wickfield is now too confused and upset to understand what has happened. The business is run by HEEP alone. I have the proof here that HEEP is a forger and a cheat[66]!'

Uriah Heep put out his hand for the paper, but Mr Micawber hit him hard with his walking stick. Heep held his hand in pain as his clerk went on speaking.

'Heep is a forger and a cheat!'

'Oh, Uriah, Uriah!' Mrs Heep cried. 'Be *humble* again, as you were before.'

'Be quiet, mother!' Heep shouted for the third time. Then he looked at us. 'I've *humbled* Mr Wickfield and his daughter. I'll *humble* all of you, too! You can't prove any of this!'

Mr Micawber held up a small black book and smiled. 'The proof is here,' he said. 'This is your private note book, Heep. You thought that you had burned it. But Mrs Micawber found it in your house. We live there, remember. In this book, there are several forgeries of Mr Wickfield's signature and of mine.' Mr Micawber smiled. 'Yes! Heep has signed papers with our names,' he said. 'He has made false accounts and signed them himself. He has stolen EVERYTHING from the firm. HEEP is a forger and a cheat!'

Uriah Heep looked across the room to the iron safe[67]. When he saw the key in the lock, he ran towards the safe and opened the door. Then he gave a loud cry.

'Where are my accounts?' he screamed. 'The accounting books have all been stolen!'

'I have them,' Traddles said quietly.' I have *all* your papers. And I have the power to keep them and show them to the court.'

Mrs Heep began to cry. She told her son over and over again to be humble and save them both. He said nothing, but now he looked angry and frightened too.

At that moment, my Aunt Betsy stood up and ran towards Uriah Heep.

'I understand everything now,' she cried. '*You* took the money that Mr Wickfield had invested for me! You took it all and I want it back!'

'My dear aunt,' I said quietly. 'Traddles will help you to get back your money.'

'Perhaps I haven't got it,' Heep said.

'But I know that you have,' Traddles replied. 'You will return all of Miss Betsy's money and the court will punish you. But now, I want you to stay in this house.'

'What if I don't want to stay?' Heep asked.

'Then you will be kept in prison until you go to court,' Traddles replied quietly.

Uriah Heep gave me one last look of hate. Then he snarled at Mr Micawber and slowly left the room.

Agnes was crying now.

'Don't worry, Miss Wickfield,' Traddles said to her. 'I shall stay here. Go to your father. Look after him. Try to make him understand that all is well. He has nothing to fear now.'

I said a few words to Agnes too and she smiled sadly.

Mr Micawber took my aunt and myself to his house. When Mrs Micawber saw her husband's smiling face, she smiled too.

'All is well, my love!' Mr Micawber cried. 'We are poor, of course, but now we can be happy! Now we must hope that something will turn up!'

'Mr Micawber,' my aunt said quietly. 'Have you and your wife ever thought of emigration – of starting a new life in Australia?'

'We have often spoken about it,' Mr Micawber replied sadly. 'But emigrants must have money, Miss Trotwood. Until something turns up, we can't –'

'Money is no problem,' my aunt said quickly. 'You have helped your friends. Soon I will have all my money again. I would be happy to give some to you.'

Mr Micawber smiled. 'I could not accept it as a *gift*,' he said, 'I will work hard in Australia and pay you back.'

'I agree,' my aunt said. 'There is another thing too. Some friend's of David are going to Australia very soon. Why don't you all go on the same ship? You may be able to help each other.'

'Mr Micawber is a good man,' Mrs Micawber said. 'Something will certainly turn up in Australia!' And she smiled happily.

'Yes, something will certainly turn up there!' Mr Micawber said. He was smiling too.

16

My Dora

And now I must remember the saddest time in my life. My Dora, my child-wife, had been ill for a long time. I could not hope that she would ever get better. Never again would my dear wife run about in our garden with her little dog, Jip.

Dora was still beautiful and she still smiled at us – my aunt and myself. But now, I never carried her downstairs. She stayed in bed and Jip stayed with her.

One evening, when I was sitting beside her, Dora began to talk about Agnes. 'Davy,' she said quietly. 'I want to see Agnes. I want to see Agnes very much.'

'I will write to her at once,' I said.

'Thank you. You are very kind to me, Davy! I really do want to speak to Agnes, you know. It's very important.'

I smiled. 'I'm sure that it is, my dear,' I said. 'And I am sure that Agnes will come.'

'Are you very lonely when you are downstairs by yourself?' Dora whispered.

'I am always lonely, my dear love, when I see your empty chair,' I said.

'My empty chair,' she repeated quietly. 'That sounds so very sad! Do you really miss me?'

'You know I do,' I replied.

'That makes me sad and happy too,' Dora whispered. 'After I have seen Agnes, I shall have nothing left to live for.'

'You must get well again, Dora.'

'Oh, Davy, sometimes I think that will never happen.'

'Don't say that my dearest Dora! Don't say that!' I replied sadly. But I knew that she was right.

Agnes arrived and, with my aunt and myself, she sat with my Dora all day. We did not talk much, but Dora was very happy. When the evening came, I sat with Dora alone. Did I know that my child-wife was dying? I knew it, but I could not believe it. I still hoped that she would get better.

I sat there, with her hand in mine.

Dora looked at me and smiled. 'I have something to say to you, Davy,' she said.

'What is it, my Dora?' I said quietly.

'I'm afraid that I was too young to marry,' she said. 'I was too young in years. And I was too young in thoughts, experience and everything. I was not ready to be a wife.'

'Then I was not ready to be a husband,' I said quickly.

'But you were clever and I never was,' Dora whispered.

'We have both been very happy, my dearest Dora,' I said.

'My young husband loved his child-wife,' she replied. 'But as time went on, he would have got tired of her. Things are better as they are.'

I shook my head. I was too upset to answer.

'Don't cry, Davy,' Dora went on. 'Do one more thing for me. I want to speak to Agnes alone. When you go downstairs, send her up to me. We must be quite alone.'

I went downstairs to Agnes and gave her Dora's message. She went up to Dora at once.

I sat down sadly. Jip was sitting by the fire too. He got up, walked slowly to the door, and looked at me.

'No, Jip, not tonight,' I said. 'You must stay with me tonight.'

The little dog walked slowly back to me. Then he lay down at my feet, gave a cry and died.

At that moment, Agnes came downstairs and opened the door. She stood there, looking at me.

'Oh, Agnes, look at poor Jip,' I said.

Agnes shook her head and pointed to the room above us. She began to cry.

'Not Dora too?' I said. 'Oh, Agnes, Agnes!'

17

The Storm

I now have to write about something terrible. I do not want to write about it, but I must. Even after all this time, I cannot think of it without sadness and terror.

After Dora died, my aunt and I left our little houses in London. I made plans to go abroad[68]. Aunt Betsy had decided to go back to her house in Dover. We both stayed in London until everything was arranged.

Soon the emigrants would be leaving for Australia. I saw the Micawbers several times and Mr Peggotty too, but I never saw Emily.

One evening, I was sitting with Peggotty and her brother. We began talking about Ham. I told them of the conversation we had had in Yarmouth.

'Ham told me that he still loved Emily,' I said. 'He wished only good things for her.

'I think that I'll write to Emily,' I went on. 'I'll tell her what

Ham said. Then perhaps she'll write to him, before she goes to Australia.'

Mr Peggotty agreed and he took my letter to his niece. In a few days, he returned with Emily's answer.

'She wants you to read it, Master Davy,' he said, 'and then send it on to Ham.'

Mr Peggotty gave me Emily's letter and I read it quickly.

I thank you for your kind words. I shall never forget them. Goodbye for ever, my dear, good friend. We shall never meet again. Thank you and God bless you.

'I'll take this letter to Ham myself,' I said. 'He must be lonely, as I am too. I think of him a lot. I can be back in London before your ship sails. Then you can tell Emily that Ham has her letter. I'll take the coach to Yarmouth tonight.'

It was the end of September and dark clouds covered the sky. The wind blew harder and harder. The closer we got to the sea, the stronger the wind blew. At times, the wind blew so hard that the coach was nearly blown off the road.

In the town itself, the air was full of sand and salt water. Everyone in the streets was looking towards the angry sea. High waves were rolling onto the beach and the noise was terrible.

I looked for Ham, but I could not find him anywhere. I went to the boat-yard, where Ham sometimes worked. A fisherman told me that Ham had gone to a nearby town.

'Don't worry about Ham,' the man told me. 'He'll never come back by sea in this bad weather.'

I went back to the inn, but I could not eat and I could not rest. I went to bed, but the noise of the wind and waves kept me awake. At last, I fell asleep.

When I awoke, it was morning and someone was banging on my door.

'There's a wreck[69], sir!' a man's voice shouted. 'A ship is breaking up! The sea is too strong for her. Come quickly, if you want to see her before she goes down!'

I quickly put on some warm clothes and ran through the crowded streets. I was soon on the beach, staring at the wild sea. The angry waves were rising up like high mountains. But where was the ship? Had it gone down already?

A fisherman shouted and pointed. And then I saw the ship. It was very near the shore. One mast[70] was broken and the great sails[71] were all torn. As the terrible sea poured over the deck, it carried everything from the ship into the angry waves. But the second mast was still standing and four men were holding onto it. One of the men was wearing a red cap over his long hair.

There was a bell on the ship. As the ship rolled, lifted and fell in the water, the bell rang. We could hear its sad sound, louder than the wind and the rain. Water poured over the ship's deck again and this time, the waves were as high as the mast. Two men were washed away. Another huge wave rolled over the deck and now only one man was left. He took off his red cap and waved it in the air. His long hair was blowing in the wind.

I heard a cry and there was Ham, running past me towards the sea. He had one rope tied round his body and he carried another rope in his hand.

'Ham!' I cried. 'Don't do it! No one can live in that sea!'

Ham stopped for a moment and held my hands. 'I must try to save him!' he shouted. 'If I die today, I die. God bless you and all my friends.'

The man with long hair was still holding onto the mast. I could not see his red cap now.

Ham ran into the water and the waves carried him away from the shore, and back again. The next wave carried him out further. Ham had nearly reached the wreck, when a great wave covered it and the ship broke in half.

Then the cruel sea carried Ham back to me. But that last great wave had been too strong for my brave friend.

I sat down beside Ham's body and covered my face with my hands. Then I heard a voice calling my name and I looked up.

'There's another body, sir,' the man said.

I followed him to where the Peggottys' old boat had stood. The wind had blown the house into pieces. And there, where little Emily and I had played together long ago, was the body of another young man. His long hair half-covered his face.

It was Steerforth. He was lying with his head on his arm, as though he was asleep.

18

Leaving England

I went back to London on the next coach. I saw Mr Micawber and told him everything.

'I want you to help me,' I said. 'If Mr Peggotty hears that Ham is dead, he will be very upset. Please try to keep the news from him. And, of course, he and Emily must not be told of Steerforth's death. That would spoil their last thoughts of England.'

'My dear Copperfield,' Mr Micawber said. 'I will make sure that they do not find out before we leave.'

The emigrants were all very busy. They were buying things and packing their bags for their journey and their new life. My aunt and Agnes helped the Micawbers. I often saw Mr Peggotty, but I never saw little Emily.

At last the emigrants' great ship was ready to sail. It stood waiting where the River Thames joined the sea. Before the ship left, Peggotty and I went down the river in a little boat. We went to say goodbye to our friends for the last time.

'My dear Copperfield, you know that I'll write to you,' Mr Micawber said. 'Friends who are far away must not be forgotten.'

'You are right,' I said, as I shook his hand. 'I shall never forget you and Mrs Micawber and your kindness to me.'

Mrs Micawber began to cry. 'I shall never leave Mr Micawber!' she said.

I said goodbye to Mr Peggotty and Mrs Gummidge, but I did not see little Emily. I was glad that they had not heard about the storm. One day they would have to know, but not now.

I looked back at the great ship from our little boat. The deck of the ship was covered with people, boxes and bags of all kinds. There were strong young men and older ones. Young women were holding their babies in their arms. Older women were crying. Children were running about everywhere.

I put my arm round my dear Peggotty, who was crying too.

Then the wind filled the sails of the great ship and it began to move away from the shore. At that moment, everyone began to cheer[72]. The emigrants waved their hats and handkerchiefs.

Then I saw little Emily on the deck. She was standing close to her uncle and his strong arm was round her shoulders.

I watched the ship sail away until it was out of sight.

And now it was my turn to leave England. Without my dear Dora, I was sad and lonely. I could not stay in the places where we had lived and loved together.

I remembered my friend Steerforth too, and the brave man who had tried to save him. I wanted to get away from all those sad memories so I decided to go abroad.

I did not stay in one place. I went from city to city. I went to Italy and then on to the high, white mountains of Switzerland. There, I cried again for my Dora. Then for the first time, I began to feel at peace.

I found a quiet little inn in a village. I knew that I would be able to write there and I decided to stay for some time.

Some letters arrived for me at the little inn and one of them was from Agnes. She wrote about her feelings of love and friendship. She told me to hope for a happier future. She was proud that I was a successful author. She also told me that hard work would help me and she wished me well with my writing.

Agnes' letter made me much happier. I answered it at once. I told Agnes that I would take her advice. And I did. I worked very hard at my third book. I walked in the mountains and became stronger and healthier. My mind became clearer too. By the time I had written half the book, I was ready to return home.

I was ready to think about the past. But I was ready to think about the future too. I knew now why I wanted to go home. I wanted to see my dear Agnes again – to see her smile and hear her sweet, loving voice.

When I was a very young man, I had chosen Dora to be my wife – my child-wife. I had loved her very much. But Dora and I had never been true partners. Dora herself had known that and now I knew it too.

Now, three years after Dora's death, I could face the truth.

I loved Agnes. I loved her as a husband loves his wife.

But all our lives, I had called Agnes 'sister'. She had accepted this. Could I tell her that my feelings had changed? Or was it too late? I did not know, but I had to find out.

I decided to return to England at once.

When I arrived in London, the first person I looked for was Thomas Traddles. My old friend was a successful barrister now. I knew that he lived in rooms near the Law Courts and I looked for him there.

I walked up the stairs to his rooms and knocked on the door.

The door opened and Traddles stood there. He looked exactly the same.

'Good heavens, it's Copperfield!' he cried. 'Come in, come in!'

'My dear Traddles! It's good to see you again,' I said.

At that moment, a pretty, happy-looking young woman came into the room.

'You know Sophy, of course,' Traddles said. 'I'm glad to tell you that we were married a month ago. I suppose that you didn't get my invitation to our wedding?'

'I'm afraid not,' I replied. 'I hope you will always be very happy.'

'Well, we certainly are now,' Traddles said. And he laughed as Sophy kissed him.

'How long are you staying in London, Copperfield?'

'I am going to Dover tomorrow,' I replied. 'My aunt is living there now and my dear Peggotty is with her.'

'Take our best wishes with you,' Traddles said. 'The best wishes of Mr and Mrs Thomas Traddles!'

I took the early coach to Dover and I was at my Aunt Betsy's house in time for tea. She was delighted to see me. Peggotty, who was now my aunt's housekeeper, cried with happiness.

'When are you going to Canterbury, David?' said Aunt Betsy, when I had told her all my news.

'I shall hire a horse and ride there tomorrow morning,' I replied. I began thinking of Agnes and of my feelings for her.

But I wanted to keep them a secret and I said nothing to my aunt.

'Mr Wickfield is an old man now,' my aunt said. 'But he is happier than he was, much happier.'

'And Agnes?' I asked quietly.

'As good and as beautiful as ever,' Aunt Betsy said. 'She has a school and it is doing well.'

'Agnes does everything well,' I said, quietly. 'Does she have … Is she going to … ?'

My aunt understood me at once. 'Agnes could have married twenty times, my dear!' Aunt Betsy replied.

'But has she …?'

'I think Agnes has made her choice, but she hasn't told me anything,' my aunt said. 'If you want to know, you must ask her yourself.'

'She is my dear sister,' I said. 'I'm sure that she will tell me.'

My aunt looked at me sadly, but she did not answer.

Early next morning, I hired a horse and rode to Canterbury. I left the horse at an inn and walked to the Wickfields' house. A new servant opened the door. I asked to see Miss Wickfield.

'Tell her it's a visitor from abroad,' I said.

I was taken upstairs. Nothing had changed. Everything was the same as it had always been. I stood in the old room that I knew so well.

Then the door opened and Agnes was there, as beautiful as ever. At first she looked very surprised – almost afraid, but then she smiled.

'My dear girl,' I said and I held her in my arms. After a time, we sat down. She talked to me of the old days – the happy times and the sad times too.

'Now tell me about yourself, Agnes,' I said at last.

'What is there to tell?' she asked, smiling at me. 'Papa is well. I have a school and that is doing well too.'

'Have you anything else to tell me, sister?' I asked her quietly. 'Have you any plans for the future?'

Agnes said nothing, but she blushed and shook her head.

That afternoon, I went for a walk in the town. In the evening, I returned to the Wickfields' house for dinner. Mr Wickfield looked much older, but he was calmer too. His fear of Uriah Heep – who was now in prison – had gone. The old man's life was very quiet and he spent most of his time in his garden.

After dinner, Agnes played the piano and I stood beside her.

'Are you planning to go abroad again?' Agnes asked me quietly as she played.

'What does my sister say about that?' I replied.

'I hope that you will not.'

'Then I shall stay,' I said. 'And you will always love me as a sister.'

Suddenly Agnes looked sad, then the look disappeared. Why was she sad? I asked myself this question as I rode home, but I could not find the answer.

19

Happiness

For two months, I stayed with my aunt and worked hard on my book. It was quiet in that pleasant place by the sea and I worked well. Sometimes, I went to see Traddles in London. Every week, I rode to Canterbury and visited the Wickfields.

Every week, I read Agnes what I had written. She laughed or cried at the story and sometimes she helped me with her advice. I knew now that I loved her, but not as a sister. I loved Agnes with my whole heart.

'My life could have been so different,' I thought.

It was now nearly Christmas. Agnes had told me nothing about her own life or of any other friends. Perhaps my aunt had been wrong. Perhaps Agnes had no thoughts of marriage. She certainly never spoke of it. If I asked her about her secret, would I upset her? Could we still be friends?

I had to know the truth.

It was a cloudy day and snow lay on the ground. The wind was very cold. My horse looked cold too, as it stood outside my aunt's house.

'I am going to Canterbury, aunt,' I said. 'It's a good day for a ride.'

'I don't think that your horse agrees with you,' Aunt Betsy replied, as she looked out of the window. 'But the ride will be good for you. You spend too many hours indoors. Reading a book is easy. But I never knew that writing one was so much hard work!'

'Aunt Betsy,' I said, 'you told me once that Agnes might be in love. Is that really true?'

'I think it is,' she replied. 'And I think that Agnes is going to be married.'

'I hope she'll be happy!' I said with a smile.

'Yes. And I hope that her husband will be too!' my aunt replied.

I remember that ride to this day. The ground was hard and the air was very cold. The sea was grey and the hills were covered with snow.

Agnes was alone because her young pupils had gone home for the holidays. She was sitting by the fire, reading.

We talked for a time about my book and we were very happy together. Then we were both silent.

'Agnes,' I said quietly. 'I think that you have a secret.

Can you tell me about it?'

She turned her head away, but said nothing.

'Dearest sister, I have been told that there is a man who loves you,' I said. 'Is that true?'

Agnes stood up and walked quickly towards the window. Then she put her hands over her face and began to cry.

'Agnes! My dear sister! What have I done?' I cried.

'Please let me go away! I can't speak to you now,' Agnes replied. 'I will tell you another time. I'll write to you.'

'Agnes, I have upset you,' I said. 'I want you to be happy, you must know that. No one wants that more than I do.'

She stopped crying and looked at me. 'If I have a secret, it is not a new one,' she said. 'I have kept it to myself for many years. I cannot tell it now.'

She began to move away, but I put my arm round her.

'Dearest Agnes, I have a secret too,' I said. 'I loved my Dora, you know I did. But when she died, you were there to help me. I went away, dear Agnes, loving you. I stayed away, loving you. And at last, I have come home, loving you!'

She was crying again now. But this time, she was crying and smiling at the same time. I held her in my arms.

'David, I have something to tell *you*,' Agnes said at last.

'What is it?' I asked.

'I have loved you all my life,' Agnes replied.

It was the afternoon of the next day when I returned to my aunt's house. My aunt was sitting by the fire, waiting for me.

'Who is that with you?' she asked. 'I can't see very well now.'

'Agnes,' I said.

My aunt looked surprised but she said nothing.

'Aunt Betsy, you told me something about Agnes,' I said. 'I asked her to tell me about it.'

'Then you shouldn't have done,' my aunt replied.

'Agnes is in love and she's very happy,' I said.

'I don't believe it!' my aunt said crossly.

'And I'm very happy too, aunt,' I said. Then I took Agnes in my arms and kissed her.

My Aunt Betsy gave a great shout and began to cry. She cried so loudly that Peggotty ran into the room. When Peggotty saw Agnes, she guessed the truth at once. She began to cry too. Then we all cried and kissed and were happy together.

Two weeks later, Agnes and I were married. My aunt and Peggotty were there, and Traddles and his Sophy too.

'Dearest husband,' Agnes said, as we drove away together. 'I have one more thing to tell you.'

'What is it, dear?' I said.

'Before Dora died, she told me that one day, I should take her place[73].'

Then Agnes cried and I cried too, but we were both very happy.

20

Afterwards

My dear Agnes and I have been married for ten years. We have five children – three girls and two boys. My Aunt Betsy is in good health and so is my dear Peggotty.

My books have sold well and made me rich and famous. I live in London, that great city where so much has happened to me. Now the bad times are far away and we are all very happy.

One spring evening, our servant told us that an old man wanted to see me.

'Let him come in,' I said.

Agnes was very surprised and stood up quickly when our visitor came into the room.

'It's Mr Peggotty!' she cried. 'You look very well! Sit down here, by the fire.'

Mr Peggotty sat down. He soon had two of our children on his knee and the others stood close by.

'These dear children are no bigger than you were, Master Davy, when you first came to my house,' Mr Peggotty said.

I smiled. 'Time has changed *me* more than you,' I said. 'You must stay with us and we'll tell you all our news.'

'And we'll hear your news too,' Agnes said. 'Have you done well in Australia?'

'Very well,' Mr Peggotty replied. 'I've been a sheep-farmer and I've kept cattle too.'

'What about little Emily?' Agnes and I both said together.

'She looks the same as ever to me,' Mr Peggotty said. 'She's never married. She's always stayed with me and Mrs Gummidge. One day, Emily found out that Ham was dead – and how he died. I had known for a year, but I had not told her. She was very quiet and very sad when she heard the news. But she went on working hard and she is better now. She's still my pretty little Emily.'

'And Mrs Gummidge?' I asked. 'Is she the same?'

'No, Master Davy, she's changed,' Mr Peggotty said, and he laughed. 'She's cheerful and always smiling now.'

'I am glad to hear it,' I said. 'We know that Mr Micawber has done well. He has paid back all the money that my aunt lent him.'

'He worked hard to get that money,' Mr Peggotty said. 'I think he worked harder than any of us. He started as a sheep-farmer too, but now the Micawbers live in the town.

'I live there too, with little Emily and Mrs Gummidge,' Mr Peggotty went on. 'Life is easier for all of us now. Mr Micawber is an important man in the town. Everyone knows Mr Wilkins Micawber! He often talks about you, Master Davy. He tells people how he and his wife looked after a poor little boy. A boy called David Copperfield, who is now the famous author. Mr Micawber often gives speeches about you and your books too!'

Mr Peggotty stayed with us for nearly a month. His sister – my Peggotty, and my aunt came from Dover to see him. We all enjoyed talking together about the old days and the time passed quickly.

I took Mr Peggotty back to Yarmouth, to see the place where Ham was buried. Mr Peggotty bent down, picked up some earth from the grave and put it in his pocket. 'For Emily,' he said quietly.

Agnes and I saw his ship sail away. We knew that we would never see him again.

And so I have come to the end of this book and the end of my story. I am happy with my dear wife, my family and my friends. Agnes is also my partner and my dearest friend.

My Aunt Betsy is eighty years old now, but she is healthy and strong. One of my daughters has her name – Betsy Trotwood – and she is my aunt's favourite.

Dear Peggotty is old too and she loves my children as much as she once loved me – her little Davy.

Thomas Traddles is a well-known barrister. His wife, Sophy, is very proud of him.

And now, as my story ends, I look up and see the face that I love. I smile. My Agnes smiles too and I am happy.

Points for Understanding

1

1 There were two visitors to the house in Blunderstone.
(a) Who were they? (b) What did they look like?

2

1 Who were David's new friends? What was unusual about their home?
2 What did you think about Mr and Miss Murdstone?

3

1 David said that his life was very unhappy. Why was that?
2 Why was David sent away to school?

4

1 Why did David hate Mr Creakle's school?
2 After the holiday, David was glad to go back to the school. Why?

5

1 After his mother's death, David's life changed. How?
2 What did David decide to do?

6

1 How was David's life different now?
2 Why did the Murdstones want David back?

7

1 David met one very pleasant person and one unpleasant one. Describe them.
2 What did David do at the end of this chapter?

8

Who were the old friends that David met?

9

1 Agnes said that Steerforth was David's 'bad angel'. Why did she say that?
2 Uriah Heep had plans. What were they?

10

1 David was in love. How did he behave?
2 Why did Ham call Steerforth 'a damned villain'?

11

1 How did Traddles get to know the Micawbers?
2 How was David going to help his aunt?

12

1 What advice did Agnes give David?
2 Uriah Heep made a mistake. What was it?

13

1 Was David's marriage to Dora a happy one?
2 Did they have any problems? If they did, what were they?

14

1 What news did Mr Peggotty get about little Emily?
2 How did he find her?
3 What were his plans for the future?

15

1 Who proved Heep's villainy?
2 How did he prove it and who helped him?
3 Miss Trotwood gave Mr Micawber some advice. What was it?

16

1 Who did Dora want to see? Why do you think she wanted to see her?
2 Why did Dora think that David would have got tired of her?

17

Two of David's friends died in this chapter. Who were they and how did they die?

18

1 Who left England in this chapter?
2 Why did they leave?
3 What was David doing in this chapter?

19

David and Agnes both had secrets. What were these secrets?

20

1 Why did David write 'now the bad times are far away'?
2 What news did Mr Peggotty bring from Australia?

Glossary

1 ***account*** (page 4)
a written or spoken report about something that has happened.

2 ***debt*** (page 4)
a situation in which you owe money to other people. If you owe money to other people, you are *in debt*. A person or company that is owed money by another person or company is called a *creditor*. A person or company that owes money is called a *debtor* and the money they owe is called a *debt*.

3 ***portrait*** (page 4)
a description of someone or something, for example in a book.

4 ***set*** – *to set* (page 4)
to write or produce a play, book, film etc that happens in a particular time or place.

5 ***public coach*** (page 4)
a *coach* is an old-fashioned vehicle that is pulled by horses. People who did not have a coach of their own, paid to travel in a *public coach*.

6 ***carrier's cart*** (page 4)
a vehicle with four wheels and no roof that is pulled by a horse and is used for carrying goods or people from one place to another.

7 ***wastes*** – *to waste something* (page 5)
to fail to make effective use of something that is valuable and could help you. James Steerforth does not make good use of the opportunities that are given to him.

8 ***ruins*** – *to ruin something* (page 5)
to destroy or severely damage something. If you have lost all of your money or power, you are *ruined*. *Ruin* is the loss of all your money or power. Later in the story, Uriah Heep says that he has saved Mr Wickfield from ruin, but this is not true.

9 ***badly treated*** – *to treat someone badly* (page 5)
to treat someone in an unfair or cruel way.

10 ***county*** (page 7)
a region that has its own local government in some countries such as the UK and US.

11 ***widow*** (page 7)
a woman whose husband has died and who has not married again. A man whose wife has died and who has not married again is called a *widower*.

12 ***bonnet*** (page 7)
a hat that ties under your chin.
13 ***expecting your child*** – *to expect a child* (page 8)
if a woman is *expecting a child*, she has a baby developing inside her body.
14 ***anxiously*** (page 9)
in a way that shows you are worried because you think something bad might happen.
15 ***cotton wool*** (page 9)
soft cotton used, for example, for cleaning a cut in your skin or removing make-up.
16 ***bowed*** – *to bow* (page 9)
to bend your body forwards from the waist, especially to show respect for someone.
17 ***dog kennel*** (page 10)
a small building where a dog sleeps and is protected from bad weather.
18 ***blush*** – *to blush* (page 10)
if you blush, your cheeks become red because you feel embarrassed or ashamed.
19 ***Master Davy*** (page 10)
Master is an old-fashioned word used for talking to or about a young boy. Davy is a friendly way of saying David.
20 ***frowned*** – *to frown* (page 11)
to move your eyebrows down and closer together because you are annoyed, worried, or thinking hard. An expression that you make in this way is called a *frown*.
21 ***waved*** – *to wave* (page 11)
to move your hand to say hello or goodbye or as a signal.
22 ***waves*** (page 14)
a line of water that rises up on the surface of a sea, lake, or river.
23 ***spoil*** – *to spoil someone* (page 15)
to always allow a child to have or do everything that they want, so that they learn to think only of themselves.
24 ***firm*** (page 15)
showing that you are in control of a situation and will not be easily forced to do something.
25 ***snarled and barked*** – *to snarl; to bark* (page 16)
if an animal such as a dog or a lion *snarls*, it makes an angry sound in its throat and shows its teeth. If a dog *barks*, it makes a short high sound.

26 ***sister-in-law*** (page 17)
the wife of your brother. The husband of your sister is your *brother-in-law*. The husband of your daughter is your *son-in-law*. You are his *father-in-law* or *mother-in-law*.

27 ***impractical*** (page 17)
Someone who is *practical* is good at making sensible decisions and choices, especially the types of decisions and choices that you have to make every day. Someone who is *impractical* is not good at this.

28 ***grateful*** (page 18)
feeling that you want to thank someone because they have given you something or have done something for you. If you are not grateful to someone who has helped you or been kind to you, you are *ungrateful*.

29 ***cane*** (page 19)
a stick used for punishing children in schools. If you punish a child by hitting them with a *cane*, you *cane* them.

30 ***twisted*** – *to twist something* (page 19)
to force something out of its original shape or position by bending it or turning it round.

31 ***handkerchief*** (page 21)
a small square piece of cloth or paper used for wiping your nose or eyes.

32 ***willing*** (page 21)
if you are willing to do something, you do it when someone asks you, sometimes when you do not want to.

33 ***inn*** (page 21)
a small hotel or pub, especially one in the countryside.

34 ***stepfather*** (page 23)
someone's stepfather is their mother's new husband in a second or later marriage.

35 ***shillings*** (page 25)
a small unit of money that was used in the UK until 1971. It was equal to five new pence.

36 ***funeral*** (page 28)
a ceremony that takes place after someone dies, usually including a religious ceremony, and the formal process of taking the body to the place where it is *buried* – put in a deep hole in the ground. The place where a dead body is *buried* is called a *grave*.

37 ***warehouse*** (page 30)
a big building where large amounts of goods are stored.

38 ***humble*** (page 30)
A home that is *humble* is simple and with only basic equipment or features. If a person is *humble*, they are not proud and do not think that they are better than other people. Later in the story, Uriah Heep often uses the word *humble* to describe himself. But he is not *humble*.

39 ***turn up*** (page 31)
to happen or appear unexpectedly or by chance. Mr Micawber hopes that an opportunity to make money will appear by chance.

40 ***beggar*** (page 32)
If you ask people for money or food, usually because you are very poor, you *beg*. Someone who is very poor and lives by asking people for money or food is called a *beggar*.

41 ***late*** (page 33)
late is used for talking about someone who has died, especially recently.

42 ***shawl*** (page 33)
a large piece of material that is worn by a woman around her shoulders or on her head.

43 ***couch*** (page 34)
a long low comfortable seat that two or three people can sit on.

44 ***hired*** – *to hire* (page 38)
if you hire something, such as a car, room, or piece of equipment, you pay the owner so that you can use it, especially for a short time.

45 ***clerk*** (page 39)
someone whose job is to look after the documents in an office, court etc. Uriah Heep wants to be a *lawyer*, like Mr Wickfield, and is studying the *law* – the system of rules within a country, region, or community dealing with people's behaviour and activities. If you want to become a lawyer, you must first become an *articled clerk*. If someone is *articled* to a company, they are employed by that company through a legal agreement while they finish their education or training. A *solicitor* is a lawyer who gives legal advice, writes legal contracts, and represents people in the lower courts of law. A *barrister* is a lawyer in England or Wales who is allowed to speak in the higher law courts.

46 ***housekeeper*** (page 39)
someone whose job is to clean someone else's house and sometimes cook their meals.

47 ***head boy*** (page 42)
a senior boy in a school who is the leader of the students and who represents the school on official occasions.

48 ***career*** (page 42)
a job or series of related jobs that you do, especially a profession that you spend a lot of your working life in.

49 ***respect*** – *to respect someone* (page 47)
to feel admiration for someone because of their personal qualities, their achievements, or their status, and show this by treating them in a polite and kind way.

50 ***civil cases*** (page 48)
A *case* is a legal matter that will be decided in a court. *Civil law* is the part of law that deals with disagreements between people rather than with crime. A *civil case* is a legal matter which is not a crime.

51 ***will*** (page 48)
a legal document that explains what you want to happen to your money and possessions after you die.

52 ***good angel*** (page 49)
a very good and kind person who is sent to help another person.

53 ***picnic*** (page 53)
a meal eaten outside, especially in the countryside.

54 ***damned villain*** (page 57)
A *villain* is an evil person, or a criminal, and evil or criminal behaviour is called *villainy*. The impolite expression *damned* is used for emphasizing what you are saying, especially when you are angry about something.

55 ***fault*** (page 57)
the fact of being responsible for a bad or unpleasant situation. If something is someone's fault, they are responsible for it.

56 ***deceived*** – *to deceive someone* (page 57)
to trick someone by behaving in a dishonest way.

57 ***invested*** – *to invest* (page 59)
to use your money with the aim of making a profit from it, for example by buying property or buying shares in a company. Money you use in this way is called an *investment*.

58 ***Parliamentary debates*** (page 61)
A *debate* is a formal discussion that ends with a decision made by voting. *Parliamentary debates* are important debates that take place in Parliament – the main law-making institution in the UK. The people who write down the words that are spoken in these debates

must write very quickly because they must write down every word accurately.

59 ***rely on*** – *to rely on someone* (page 64)
to trust someone or something to do something for you.

60 ***accounts*** (page 71)
a detailed record that a person or business keeps of the money they receive and spend in a particular period of time. Later in the story, Uriah Heep is accused of making *false accounts* – keeping records of money he and Mr Wickfield have received and spent that are not true.

61 ***emigrating*** – *to emigrate* (page 76)
to leave your country in order to live in another country. Someone who leaves their country to live in another country is an *emigrant* and the process of leaving one country to live in another country is called *emigration*.

62 ***fraud*** (page 78)
the crime of obtaining money from someone by tricking them, or the action of producing false documents or information in order to get what you want.

63 ***justice*** – *to bring someone to justice* (page 79)
to make someone have a *trial* (an examination in a court of law) in order to find out whether they are guilty of a crime.

64 ***prove*** – *to prove something* (page 79)
to provide evidence that shows that something is true. Evidence that shows that something is true is called *proof*.

65 ***act for*** – *to act for someone* (page 80)
if you act for someone, you do something as their representative.

66 ***a forger and a cheat*** (page 81)
A *forger* is a criminal who makes copies of valuable documents or works of art, or of other people's signatures. The copies a *forger* makes are called *forgeries*. A *cheat* is someone who behaves dishonestly, or does not obey rules.

67 ***safe*** (page 83)
a strong metal box with a special lock, used for storing valuable things. The safe in this story is made of *iron*, a hard heavy metal that is very strong.

68 ***abroad*** – *to go abroad* (page 87)
to go to a foreign country

69 ***wreck*** (page 89)
an occasion on which a ship sinks

70 ***mast*** (page 89)
a tall pole that the *sails* hang from on a ship.

71 ***sail*** (page 89)
A *sail* is a large piece of strong cloth used for catching wind to move a boat or ship across water.

72 ***cheer*** (page 91)
to give a loud shout of happiness or approval.

73 ***take someone's place*** (page 98)
to be in the position that another person was in. Dora wanted Agnes to be David's wife after she died.

Macmillan Education
4 Crinan Street
London N1 9XW
A division of Springer Nature Limited
Companies and representatives throughout the world

ISBN 978–1–3800–3797–8

This version of David Copperfield by Charles Dickens was retold by Elizabeth Walker for Macmillan Readers

First published 2008

This edition published 2019

Illustrated by John Dillow and Martin Sanders
Cover photo Alamy Stock Photo/John Reddy

Printed and bound in Thailand

2023 2022 2021 2020 2019
10 9 8 7 6 5 4 3 2 1